ELVIS

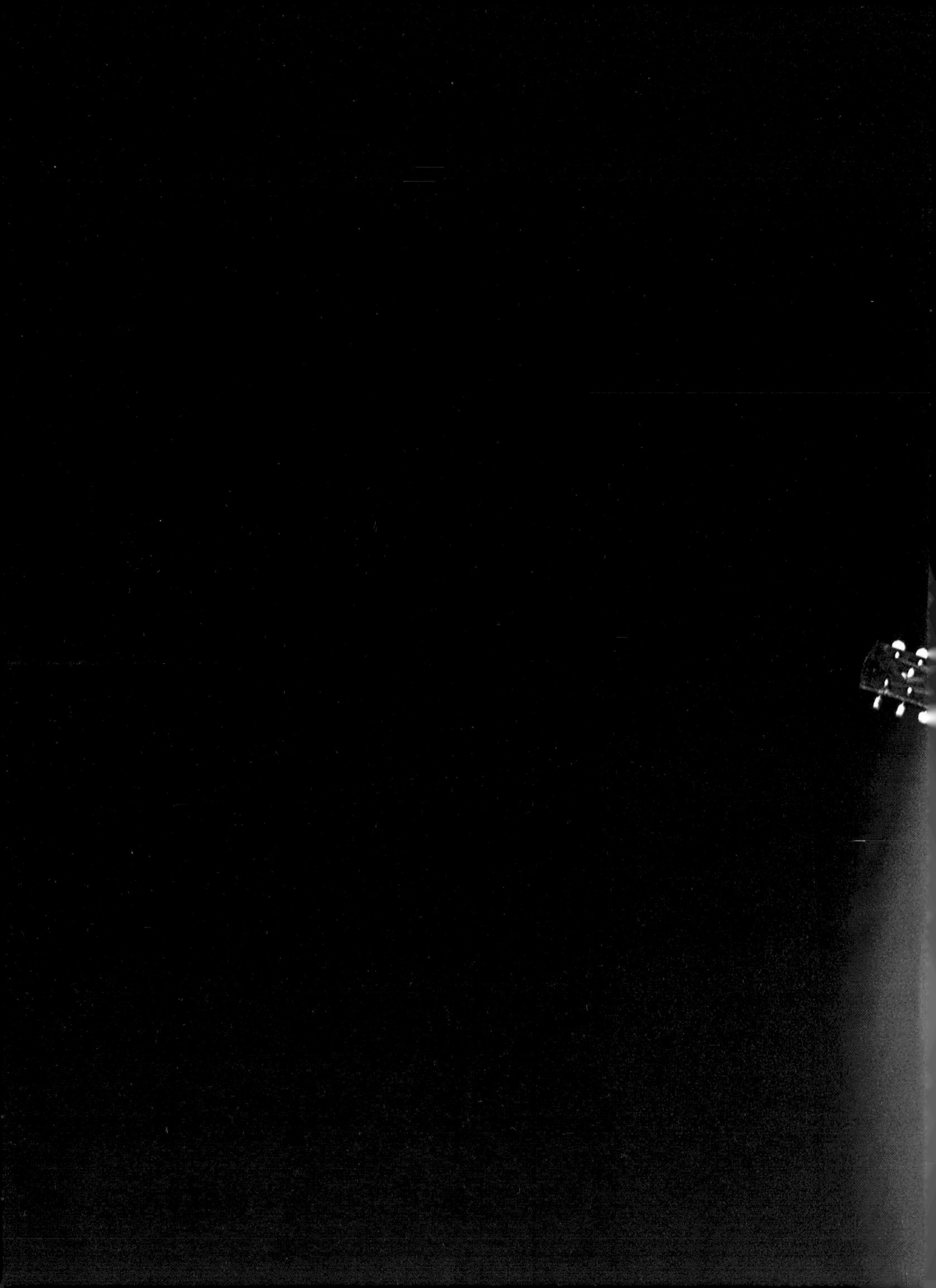

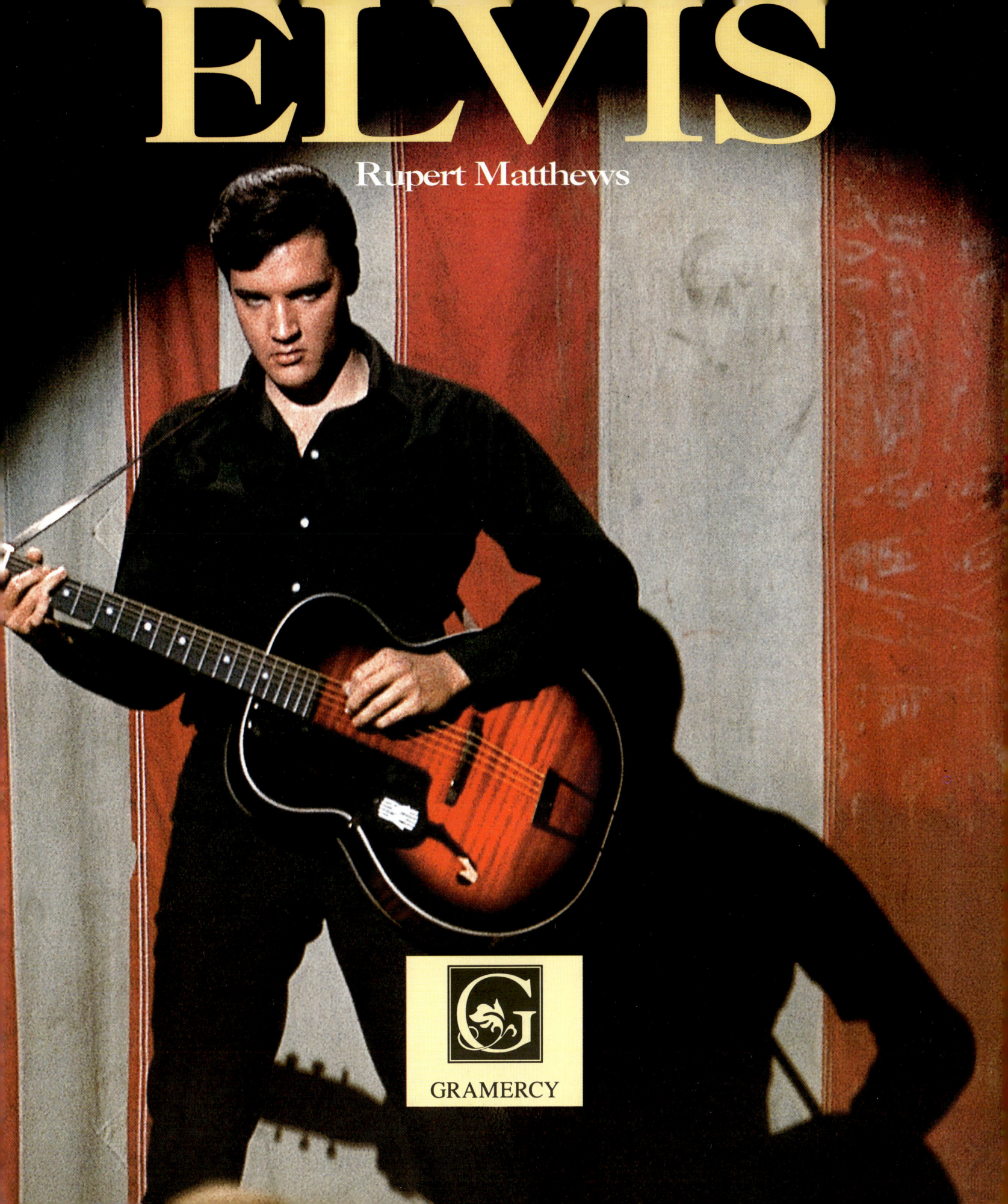

Copyright © 1998 Regency House Publishing Limited

No part of this book may be reproduced or transmitted in any form or by any means electronic or mechanical including photocopying, recording, or by any information storage and retrieval system, without permission in writing from the publisher.

This 1998 edition is published by Gramercy Books, a division of Random House Value Publishing, Inc.,
201 East 50th Street, New York, NY 10022

Gramercy Books and colophon are trademarks of Random House Value Publishing, Inc.

Random House New York • Toronto •London • Sydney • Auckland
http: / / www.randomhouse.com/

Printed in Italy

ISBN 0-517-16053-6

10 987654321

CONTENTS

INTRODUCTION	8
CHAPTER ONE THE BOY FROM TUPELO	11
CHAPTER TWO INTO THE LIMELIGHT	20
CHAPTER THREE THE PELVIS	32
CHAPTER FOUR HITTING THE BIG TIME	44
CHAPTER FIVE G.I. BLUES	54
CHAPTER SIX A CAREER IN MOVIES	65
CHAPTER SEVEN THE COMEBACK	87
CHAPTER EIGHT ELVIS LIVES	101
INDEX	110

This book constitutes the private view of the author and is not an officially sanctioned biography.

All photographs are reproduced by kind permission of Todd Slaughter of the Elvis Presley Fan Club of Great Britain.

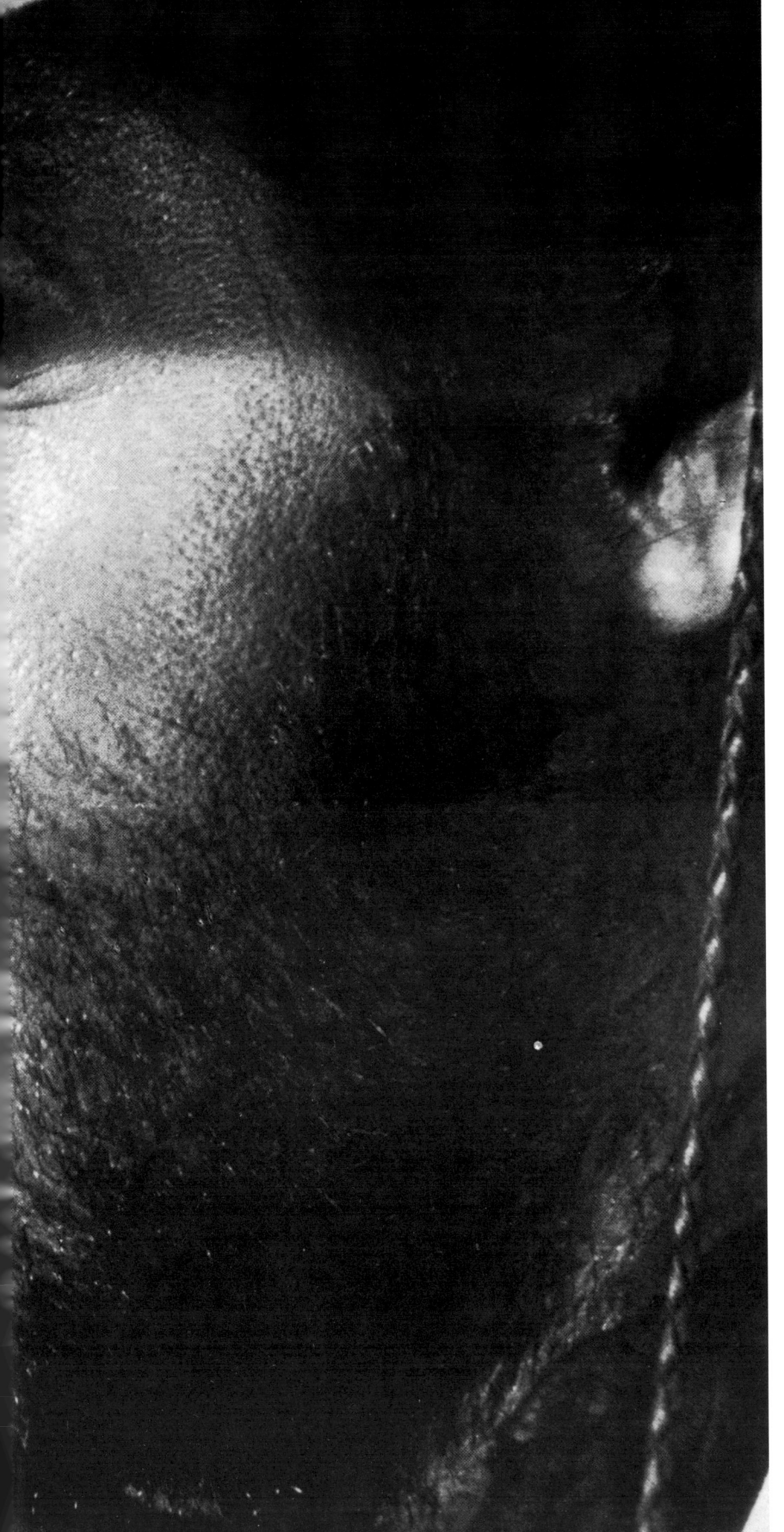

Elvis sports a rare beard in the movie *Charro*. In it, Elvis assumed what was for him an unusual role, in an attempt to prove his acting abilities to largely unsupportive critics. Elvis plays the outlaw Jess Wade who is attempting to turn over a new leaf and lead a more honest life in a small Western town. He is frustrated in his attempts when members of his old gang, led by actor Victor French, turn up to pillage the town.

INTRODUCTION

*'What kind of singer are you?' 'I sing all kinds.' 'Who do you sound like?'
'I don't sound like nobody.'*

The above brief exchange between Memphis Recording Service receptionist Marion Keisker and young truck driver Elvis Presley is possibly the most momentous in the history of popular music.

The Memphis Recording Service was run by record producer Sam Phillips and locals could come in and record a single for just $4. Customers ranged from local dance bands to others wishing to send a recorded message to distant relatives. It was in August 1953 that Elvis arrived with his guitar, intending to record a couple of songs.

Once he was settled in the studio by Keisker, who set the sound levels, Presley began to belt out *My Happiness*, an old Ink Spots number. Within seconds of Elvis starting to sing, Marion Keisker realized that here was something different and far superior to anything she had heard before. She began to scrabble about for a spare tape and managed to get one in the machine by the time Elvis was halfway through the song. When he began *That's When the Heartaches Begin*, Keisker was already recording and managed to capture the entire song. It was these recordings which would eventually put Elvis on the road to stardom.

As with so much to do with Elvis's early career, however, the facts of that recording session have become enshrined in legend.

Marion Keisker vividly remembered Presley's visit and always claimed that the record was cut as a birthday present for Elvis's mother. That would have put the session back in April. Elvis, however, later recalled, 'I paid my four bucks to the lady, because I had a notion to find out what I really sounded like. I had been singing all my life, and I was kind of curious.' According to him, the date was indeed somewhere in August.

Even the fate of the disc is unclear. Elvis said that his mother 'played it over and over until it was plumb near worn out'. These direct-cut discs were laid on to soft acetate which could only be played about 100 times before the steel needle of the record players of the time ground the grooves smooth. However, an early acetate of *My Happiness* and *That's When the Heartaches Begin* was found in 1988 among some junk in the house of Ed Leek, a friend of Elvis in the early days. According to Leek, Elvis brought the record over after the recording session, played it a few times and then left it there. 'I sounded like someone banging a trash-can lid,' commented Elvis dismissively.

Clearly accounts of this first recording are quite at odds with one another. Perhaps Elvis visited the studios twice, once to cut a disc for his mother's birthday, a disc which was soon worn out by constant playing, and then again to make another with less satisfactory results. Or Marion Keisker and Elvis may simply have recalled different versions of the same visit; but whenever it was, Elvis took his disc and left, and Marion Keisker could not forget him. She had made a note of his address and a neighbour's telephone number, and lost little time in persuading her boss, Sam Phillips, to listen to the tape. The recordings had an amateur feel to them which was hardly surprising as Elvis finished the session in about 20 minutes and accompanied himself on the guitar in a single take. But the unique qualities of Elvis's voice were more than obvious and the range and control of the voice were amazing, given the circumstances.

Sam Phillips, owner of the Memphis Recording Service, ran a small record label called Sun, producing discs of local bands for the Southern market. He had long impressed on his staff exactly what he was looking for in a recording artist. 'If I could find a white man who had the Black voice and Black sound, I could make a million dollars,' was one of his favourite sayings and with good reason. Black music had a long history of success in the Southern states, and occasionally further north and west, but racial prejudice was rife. No black singer, no matter how good, could ever be accepted in the prestigious venues as anything other than a curiosity. But it was a different story where white singers were concerned. If Phillips were only able to combine the two, he would have a gold mine and he knew it. It was this quality which Marion Keisker thought she had discovered in Elvis, but Phillips remained unimpressed. He did not call Presley.

Some months later, however, fate intervened. Sam Phillips came across a slow ballad called *Without You* recorded by another small studio, Peer Music of Nashville. He was much taken by the song, but the recording was

Elvis with his mother Gladys and father Vernon in the earliest days of his success. When, because of an injured back, he had to leave work in 1954, Vernon told Elvis, 'I never expected to be the greatest man in the world, but I wanted to be a good husband to your mother and a good father to you. Now it seems we're in for some real hard times.' He had not counted on his son's talents.

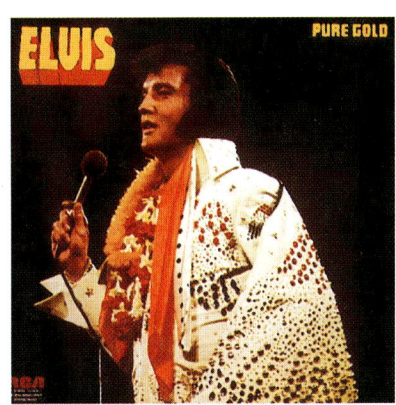

Introduction

OPPOSITE

Bizarrely, Elvis's good looks went unremarked through most of his teen years. 'The girls didn't go for me,' said Elvis, recalling his days at the L. C. Humes High School. Looking back at those times, the same girls must have been amazed at their lack of interest.

BELOW

Elvis practises harmonies with his early backing group, the Jordanaires. The group joined the Elvis team at RCA in July 1956 when Neal Matthews, Hoyt Hawkins and Hugh Jarrett joined Gordon Stoker. Stoker had earlier helped with some backing vocals on the classic *Heartbreak Hotel* in January of that year.

not of a good enough quality to release professionally. He contacted Peer Music to ask the black singer to come over for a proper recording session. Sadly for the singer, nobody at Peer had noted his address and they were unable to contact him. That was when Marion Keisker suggested Phillips call Presley.

It was noon on 26 June 1954 when the phone rang in Elvis's neighbour's house. Taking the call, Elvis was astonished to hear Phillips asking him to come over and record a song for professional release. 'I ran all the way,' Elvis recalled later. 'I was there by the time they hung up the phone.'

Unfortunately Elvis's performance failed to match his enthusiasm. The ballad, *Without You*, a slow, complex number, was not really the young Elvis's style at all. Phillips was puzzled: Marion Keisker had been so insistent that the boy had star quality that Phillips was expecting to hear something rather more convincing.

After many hours of repeated takes Phillips, in desperation, asked Elvis to do some numbers of his own choosing and the result was a very different, even startling performance. Elvis thundered out a collection of country, blues and movie songs which obviously vastly appealed to him; once a song had captured Elvis's imagination, the rest was sheer brilliance. Phillips later said, 'Man this was just Elvis on a guitar, and he could wail the heck out of a guitar. I heard him and that was it.'

Phillips wasted no time in contacting professional musicians whom he considered would collaborate well with Elvis. He even began to give some thought to the types of radio shows he would begin to bombard with discs of his new protégé: Elvis's professional career had begun and the rest, as they say, is history.

But who was the new phenomenon and where had his musical skills come from?

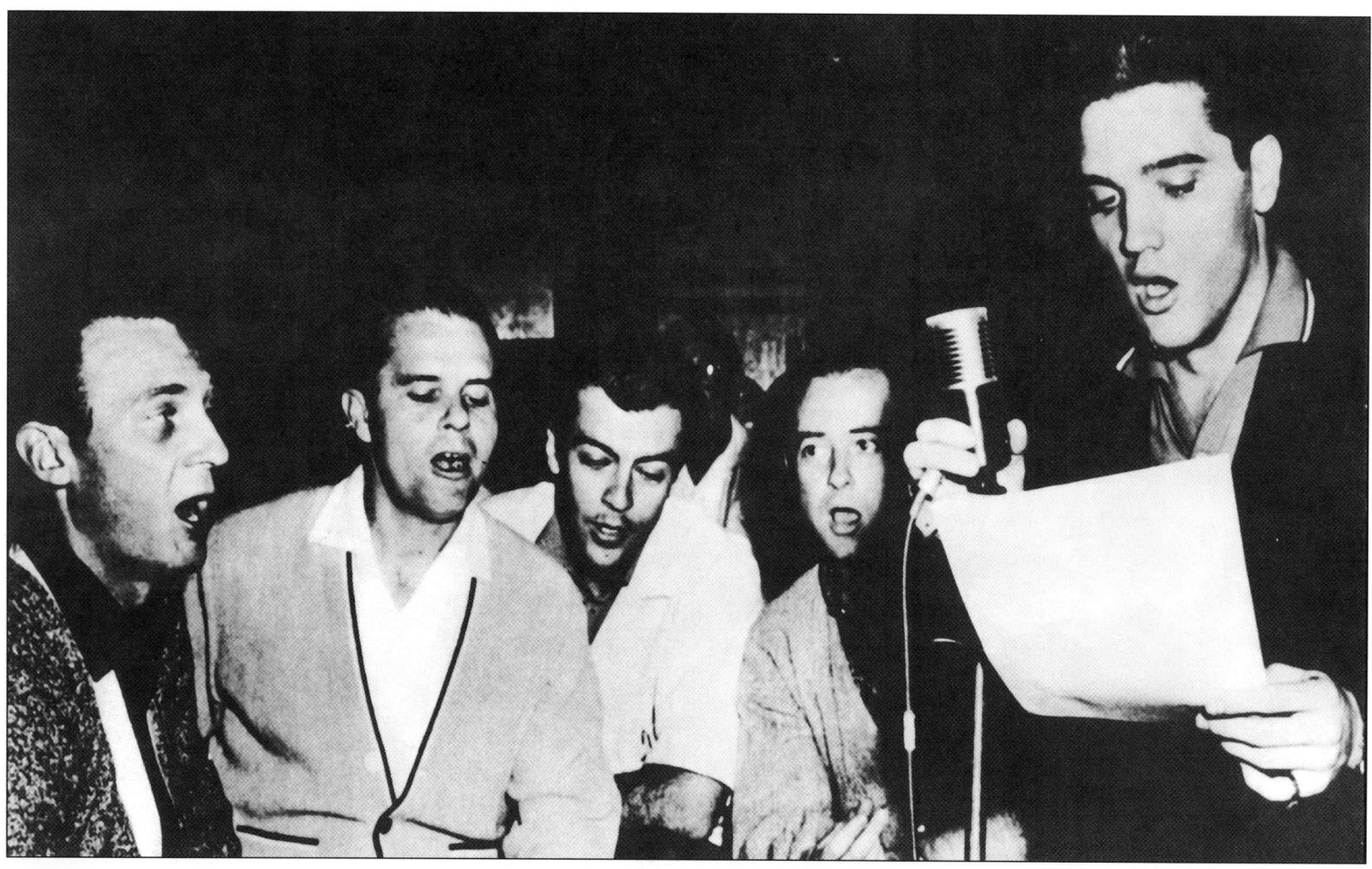

CHAPTER ONE
THE BOY FROM TUPELO

Elvis was born into a life of utter poverty in the tiny town of Tupelo, Mississippi in circumstances which, even for such a poor white family as the Presleys, was far from auspicious.

It was 8 January 1935 and icy rain had been falling for most of the night. Gladys Love Smith Presley had been having a difficult labour for many hours and was almost unconscious. At 4 a.m. she finally gave birth to a stillborn boy. However, the doctor was surprised to realize that the labour was not yet over when another baby was born half an hour later to be named Elvis Aaron. Next day his dead twin, Jesse Garon Presley, was buried in an unmarked grave and for the rest of his life, Elvis held strongly to the belief that Jesse was in heaven watching over him.

Presley's parents, Gladys and Vernon, were typical of their class and it was a constant struggle to avoid being categorized as the 'poor white trash' scorned by all facets of society. As God-fearing, church-going and honest folk, their lives were hard but respectable. Gladys and Vernon met at the church of the Assembly of God, where Gladys was the more regular attender. Although Vernon was only 17 and Gladys 21, they eloped only a few months after their first meeting, marrying in Gladys's home town of Pontotoc, before eventually returning to

Tupelo. Vernon worked at a succession of casual jobs on local farms before getting a steady job with a dairy company.

With his new job, Vernon Presley was able to scrape together $180 to buy a stack of timber and together with his father, brother and other members of his family, built a modest house measuring just 30 x 15ft (9 x 4.5m). Although the shack stood in the garden of Vernon's father's house, it was a separate family home and even boasted a small porch complete with steps up from the street and a swinging bench, indicating that there was a strong desire for respectability.

The same desire made churchgoers of the Presleys that would provide an outlet for Elvis's musical gifts, at least to his mother's ears. Even before he could talk properly, Elvis could sing. Quiet, even bored during the sermons and prayers, Elvis would leap to his feet as soon as the music began. He would hum and burble along to the hymns and, unless his mother kept a tight rein of him, would dance up and down the aisles.

Elvis later claimed that Southern gospel music was the most important influence in forming his style. *'When I was four or five,'* Elvis later told an interviewer, *'All I looked forward to was Sundays when we could all go to church. I loved the old church, filled with sunlight. This was the only singing training I had – I never had lessons. I'd just try to sing as loud and in tune as I could. I was always singing. People living on the same housing lot as me would stop and listen.'* In fact, Elvis loved music so much he sometimes slipped away after church to attend other services. He was particularly drawn to churches frequented by black people, though as a white kid was shy of entering them. Instead, he would sit outside listening to the gospel songs floating through the open windows.

But it was not just the music that impressed itself on Elvis. He recalled the way both ministers and singers used their bodies in an entirely natural way to emphasize the beat and rhythm of the music as well as the underlying message of the words. 'The preachers would duck up all over the place, jumping on the piano and moving every which way,' Elvis later remarked. 'I guess I learned a lot from them.' That his infamous hip movements had their origins in religious expression may seem bizarre – after all, when Elvis became famous, many churchmen were outraged by his pelvic thrusts. But the idea of relinquishing oneself with vocal and bodily abandon to the music would not have been foreign to the more dynamic and charismatic of Southern circuit of gospel preachers.

It was all the more shocking, given the determined respectability of the impoverished Presley family, when Vernon Presley was arrested in November 1937. A cheque written by his employer had been tampered with to show an extra $10. The alteration had not been skilfully made and was immediately spotted by the bank. Circumstancial evidence pointed to Vernon, as well as two men with whom he worked closely, and all three were found guilty and sentenced to three years in prison.

Vernon's imprisonment shattered the family finances. Gladys could no longer afford to remain in the tiny shack where Elvis had been born, so mother and son moved in with Vernon's father. Elvis and his mother shared a room and some believe Elvis's later inability to relate to women of his own age can be traced to this period. Lacking a father figure, and with a strong mother already obsessively proud of and protective towards him, Elvis was growing up in what would now be called a dysfunctional household.

People who knew the Presleys at this time comment on the closeness of mother and son though Vernon's misdemeanours made him

'He was always lugging around his beat-up guitar and singing gospel songs or slow hill-billy ballads in a plaintive baritone,' remarked one of Elvis's teachers in his last year at school. He later developed his singing voice, achieving a remarkable range and, as seen here, was able to purchase some better guitars.

somewhat of an outsider to his own family. But the case should not be overstated. The Presley family was a large one with several male relatives able to act as father figures in Elvis's eyes and in any case, Vernon was released after about a year due to the extreme poverty of his wife and son.

When America entered the Second World War, Vernon found himself excused military service due to his prison record. But with many young men away and the war demanding tanks, aircraft and other equipment, jobs were easier to come by and were better paid. Before long, Vernon was able to purchase the type of consumer goods most families craved and prime among these were an old green Plymouth automobile and a radio. Elvis loved them both. His life-long love affair with cars, motorbikes

The Boy from Tupelo

'When I'd stand at the door, I'd see this tall, lanky boy hanging around with his nose glued to the window like a kid at a candy store,' recalled a worker at Lansky's, Elvis's favourite clothing store. It was the way Elvis dressed which shocked those who met him in those early days.

and anything on wheels may well have began with this old and battered vehicle.

'I used to listen quite a lot, and I loved records by Sister Rosetta Thorpe and country singers like Roy Acuff, Ernest Tubbs, Ted Daffan, Jimmie Rodgers, Jimmy Davies and Bob Wills,' said Elvis later on, revealing a strand of musical influence which was a strong factor in developing his talents.

It was probably on the radio that Elvis first heard the song *Old Shep* by Red Foley. As with the gospel singers who performed in church, Elvis had a great facility for picking up lyrics and melodies and his teacher at elementary school, Mrs Oleta Grimes, heard him singing the song at school one day. She was so impressed that she arranged for the 10-year-old Elvis to enter the talent contest at the Mississippi Farm and Dairy Show on 3 October 1945 – his first public performance. He did well, winning the second prize of $5 as well as receiving free rides at the fairground.

A few months after this success, on his 11th birthday, Elvis got his first guitar. Elvis's Uncle Luther was a gifted amateur musician who produced arrangements of hymns for whatever odd collection of instruments the local church had available. He taught Elvis the basics of the guitar, a few chords, and several simple tunes. After that, Elvis quickly managed to pick up tunes from the radio and became almost as adept as his uncle.

But Vernon was about to let the family down again. In September 1948, when Elvis was 13, Vernon was arrested once more though this time the crime was much less serious – he had been caught selling moonshine whiskey. Although it was illegal, most country folk enjoyed moonshine and distilleries already existed which had long and honourable histories of producing it. Clearly, the local judge did not feel Vernon's crime warranted harsh punishment and, despite his earlier, uncompleted sentence, Vernon was not sent to prison. Instead he was told to get out of town and not come back.

'We left Tupelo overnight,' said Elvis later. 'Dad packed all our belongings in boxes and put them on the top and in the trunk of our Plymouth. Then we headed for Memphis.' The move proved to have a lasting effect on Elvis in more ways than one.

For someone coming from a small country town of just 6,000 residents, the city of Memphis, with its population of 300,000, was overwhelming. Elvis grew rather shy and reserved, finding it difficult to make friends easily. It did not help matters that the Presleys could afford only a single room, sharing both kitchen and bathroom with three other families. Vernon was having trouble keeping a job, so Gladys went to work as a waitress. It is thought the family's income averaged just $35 a week.

In 1949 matters improved: Vernon finally

Elvis

The heavy but fragile microphones of the early 1950s were giving way to lighter and more robust equipment as Elvis made his stage debut. This liberated Elvis from having to remain stationary when singing and allowed him to display the famous pelvic action to its full effect.

The Boy from Tupelo

RIGHT

'I wanted to be different, to look older and be noticed. The only way I could do it was with sideburns and black clothes.' Although Elvis later abandoned these for brighter colours, striking black outfits predominated in the early years.

OPPOSITE

The famous hip-shaking walk goes into action. It was these rhythmic and hypnotic gyrations which so shocked Middle America when Elvis performed them on the Milton Berle Show. 'Uncle Miltie' was to be castigated in over 700,000 letters for allowing such a display on his family show.

got a full-time job and was able to move his family into a three-room apartment. Although it was a federal housing project, it was away from Poplar Avenue, the poorest white area in Memphis. The move enabled Elvis to go to the L.C. Humes High School, a whites-only school which prided itself on giving a solid education to the children of poorer families in order that they could get good honest jobs. The only drawback was that the education was very basic and covered only six subjects which could in any way be termed academic. Most boys were encouraged to take classes in 'shop' and 'commercial', while the girls were taught 'home economics'.

At first, Elvis did not make much of an impression. One girl at L.C. Humes recalled Elvis arriving. 'He was a very shy person, but he did carry this guitar with him.' The guitar was rarely idle, with Elvis taking every opportunity to pick out a tune and practise his singing. He performed at a nearby Veterans' Hospital, making friends with another musically talented pupil, Red West, although West was in the year below Elvis.

By the age of 16, Elvis's talents were beginning to get him noticed, and so was his appearance. In the autumn of 1950, Elvis got a job at Loew's State Theater where he earned $12.60 for five shifts of five hours. Although Elvis handed all his earnings over to his mother, she gave him some back and one of his favourite places for spending money was Lansky Brothers on Beale Street. This was a tough black area where few whites ventured; but Elvis knew the place which he had visited to hear gospel and blues music. The attraction for Elvis were the clothes. Nowhere else in Memphis could he find pink shirts, yellow trousers and other outrageously coloured items. To make himself even more conspicuous, Elvis took to growing his hair long and slicking it back with gel to form a DA style. 'Elvis stood

out like a camel in the Arctic,' recalled one fellow pupil years later.

Maybe it was because of Elvis's outlandish appearance that some of the tougher kids at school picked on him. One day, three boys hustled Elvis into the boys' lavatories and produced a pair of scissors. The hair, they declared, was coming off and Elvis was going

The Boy from Tupelo

Elvis in the laid-back, Western-style clothing he adopted for his successful first movie, *Love Me Tender*. In it, Elvis plays a Texas farm boy caught up in a web of family jealousies and feuds set against the background of the Civil War.

to have a crew-cut like most regular guys. Fortunately Red West appeared in the nick of time. Red was a large fellow, one of the leading figures on the school football team and was accordingly respected by his fellow pupils. He saved Elvis's hair, which Elvis would never forgot and which later on earned Red a place in his entourage.

Another school friend later employed by Elvis was Marty Lacker. Like Red West, Lacker had musical aspirations; but though he loved the local music scene, he did not have the talent

of West, let alone Elvis. His particular skill lay in getting along with people and always managing to remember what needed doing and when.

In December 1952, the annual L.C. Humes Minstrel Show took place. Red West and two other musical pupils put together an act for the show, but Elvis declined to take part, his shyness appearing to have got the better of him. However, the history teacher, Miss Scrivener, had other ideas. She had heard Elvis pick out tunes for his own pleasure or for the entertainment of fellow students and tried her best to encourage Elvis to perform. By the time Red West and his group had finished playing, it was still uncertain that Elvis would go on stage. Then he moved forward, his old guitar in his hand, looking far from impressive and clearly in some trepidation of what he was about to do.

'Then it happened,' said Red West. *'Elvis put one foot up on a chair to act as a prop, and he started to plunk away at the tune* Old Shep. *Then he whipped into a fast song, then a ballad. When he finished his show, the kids went crazy. They applauded and applauded. They just went mad. He seemed to be amazed that for the first time in his life someone other than his family really liked him. At last, it seemed, he had found a way to make outsiders love him. As shy as he was, he had a definite magic on stage.'*

Suddenly, Elvis had achieved popularity. His fellow pupils now recognized him as a skilled musician, even if his name had been misspelled Prestly in the programme. He was no longer threatened or intimidated but was accepted into many of the informal groups which existed among the pupils. He was not able to stay completely out of trouble, however. He managed to lose his evening job at the theatre after he and another boy got into a fight over one of the girls selling candy to customers.

Elvis left school in June 1953 and took the first job he could find, as a factory hand at the Precision Tool Company. However, he clearly aimed to better himself; after a few months, and taking a pay cut of $6 a week, he went to work for the Crown Electric Company so that he could attend night classes to train as an electrician. He had confided to a friend what he was expecting out of life – to work with cars – adding a comment which, with hindsight, contained a certain irony. 'I don't need that much money,' he said, 'just enough for me and Mama to get by.'

It was while driving a delivery tuck for Crown Electric that Elvis spotted the Memphis Recording Service studios. Flushed with confidence from his recent success, Elvis decided to cut a disc for his mother and with this in mind entered the recording studio where he met Marion Keisker and her boss Sam Phillips.

An uncharacteristically careless Elvis. In his early days Elvis was careful to appear well groomed in his favourite black or pink outfits. Such shots were taken only when Elvis was off-guard and not expecting to be photographed.

CHAPTER TWO
INTO THE LIMELIGHT

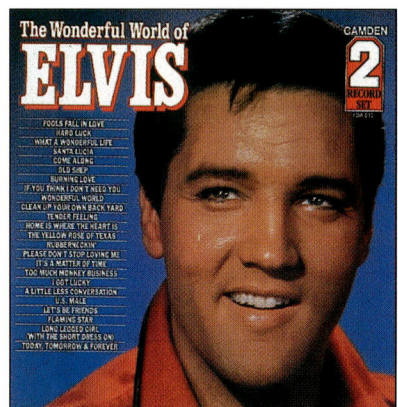

At the finish of Elvis's studio performance before Sam Phillips on 26 June 1954, the first man Phillips contacted was Scotty Moore. Phillips had often discussed with him his plan of finding a white boy with a black voice, and Moore had enthusiastically concurred. Although he played guitar with a country band called the Starlight Wranglers, Moore was willing to take on other jobs and was keen to develop new styles. He agreed to meet the new discovery with the prospect of working with him in the future.

The next Sunday morning, Elvis telephoned Moore's house to arrange a time to meet and to ask instructions for finding the place. Moore's wife, who spoke to Elvis, thought he sounded a nice polite young man but, when opening the door to Elvis that afternoon, got something of a shock. For his first meeting with professional musicians, Elvis had chosen his clothes with care, in the hope that he would soon be forming an association with them. He wore a pink shirt, black-and-pink striped trousers and white shoes.

Scotty Moore and Elvis began to work through a few songs, including *I Apologise, I Don't Hurt Anymore* and *That's All Right*. Moore's bass player, Bill Black, came by after a while, curious to hear Phillips's hot new singer. After some hours, the session broke up and Scotty Moore phoned Phillips. Although he was not sure quite what to make of Elvis, Moore told Phillips that he considered it worth booking the boy in for a proper recording session. It was clear that Elvis had a fine voice, but his diffident behaviour was at odds with both his clothes and his musical style. Moore had no idea what songs to suggest that Elvis should sing.

The recording session in Phillips's professional studio was booked for the evening of Monday 6 July. Bill Black again provided the bass accompaniment to Moore's lead guitar and Elvis's voice. The trio began with *Harbor Lights*, an old ballad recently revived by Sammy Kaye. The recording was not up to much, being too restrained and rough-edged. They moved onto *I Love You Because*, with no more success than before. Time was passing and Phillips was beginning to be concerned, giving the trio a break period while he listened to the tapes to try to work out where improvements could be made.

Elvis making a recording at the studios of RCA. His first efforts revealed his inexperience; at times, his voice seemed to fade almost to nothing in the middle of a chorus, a result of his moving his head away from the microphone to encourage the band. Useful on stage, such tactics were unsuited to the studio, a fact which soon became evident to Elvis.

After a few minutes, Elvis began to strum *That's All Right*. The two professionals joined in to recreate the private session which had already taken place at Scotty Moore's house. Elvis was on top form as he threw his heart into the song and his body into the performance. Sitting in the control room, Phillips was galvanized and ran through to the studio. 'What the devil are you boys doing?' he is said to have demanded. 'Don't know,' replied Elvis. 'Well find out real quick,' shouted Phillips, 'and let's put it on tape.'

The song was reworked before taping and was followed by *Blue Moon of Kentucky* as the B side of the single. Recording in the mid-1950s was then a very different process than it is today. The electronics in the average studio, although advanced for the time, were crude by present standards. There were no banks of sliders and dials allowing the studio engineer to mix and fade different instruments. Nor was it usual to splice together elements from different takes, multi-tracking tapes being non-existent. Basically, the engineer set the levels for each microphone to get a good blend of the different instruments and vocals. Then the band played it through and that was it.

Very different also was the speed of the operation. A small label like Sam Phillips's Sun Records served a relatively small area with local music and talent. With a nearby pressing factory, it was easy to get a finished disc in the shops within a few weeks. When something special came up, the process could work even faster. Elvis saw his first single hit the shops just 12 days after he recorded it.

The reason for the haste was the enormous public response to Sam Phillips's publicity drive. The day after the recording session, Phillips ran off an acetate disc, similar to the one Elvis had recorded for his mother. He took it to WHBQ, a Memphis radio station which had a rhythm and blues show called *Red Hot and Blue*. The DJ, Dewey Phillips, knew his namesake Sam well and agreed to listen to it and, having heard Elvis, was eager to play the disc on his show the next night.

Sam hurried back and excitedly told his new band to listen to the radio the next evening. By the time the show started, however, Elvis was too nervous to listen and went out to the movies to see a Western. When the record was played, the effect was electric. Dozens of listeners called in to demand that the song be repeated. Dewey Phillips played the Elvis number again, only to be bombarded by even more calls.

One of Elvis's school friends recalled the evening clearly: *'My mom was all excited and called out to me to come in and listen to the radio as a boy from my school was singing. I knew it had to be Elvis. He was the only one whose singing was worth a damn.'*

Back at WHBQ, Dewey Phillips was beginning to get worried. Many of the callers had assumed Elvis to be black. If that idea caught on, Elvis might find himself involved in all kinds of misunderstanding. Phillips called Sun Records to ask Elvis to come in for an interview. As *That's All Right* went out over the airwaves yet again, Sam Phillips raced round to Elvis's home only to find he had gone out. Gladys eventually found her son and dragged him out of the movies to appear live on radio.

When Elvis got to the radio studio he was clearly nervous and uncertain of himself. 'Just don't say nothing dirty,' advised Dewey Phillips. Realizing that the new star was a little uptight at the prospect of being interviewed, the DJ decided not to tell him when the microphone went live. Instead he just chatted to Elvis in the studio as if to get background information ready for the interview. Only when the station returned to playing music did Elvis discover that he had been live, on air. He almost fainted.

By the end of July, *That's All Right* had reached the number 3 slot in the Memphis Country Music Charts. At that time there was no such thing as rock and roll, never mind a separate chart. Elvis slotted more easily into the country music charts because he was from Memphis than for any other reason. Keen to capitalize on this success, the musical set-up was formalized. Elvis signed a recording contract with Sun Records, while management was put into the hands of Scotty Moore.

Moore quickly made the most of his contacts in the Memphis music scene by booking the new trio into a live show at the Overton Park Shell. This was a concert of country music with the established star Slim Whitman as the main act. Needing a name by which to call themselves, the trio came up with Hillbilly Cat and the Blue Moon Boys. It was hardly a snappy title, but neatly emphasized

Elvis's small-town roots and the strong blues content of their music.

The show took place on 10 August, with two performances. During the more sedate afternoon show, Elvis sang his first success, *Old Shep*, and the song he had recorded for his mother's birthday *That's When the Heartaches Begin*. The performance was reasonably well received, but made no great impact. By the evening, however, Elvis had decided to liven his act up by playing his current hit, *That's All Right*, together with the lively rhythm and blues song, *Good Rockin' Tonight*. It proved to be an inspired decision.

Elvis made a spectacular entrance when he came on stage wearing an outrageous pink-and-white cowboy outfit. But when he began to thump out the lyrics and gyrate to the beat, the younger element of the audience went wild. The reception was nothing short of incredible. As they came off, Elvis remarked to Scotty on the volume of screaming and shouting. 'It's because you're wiggling your legs,' said Scotty. Elvis recalled what happened next. 'I went back out again, and I did a little more wiggling. And the more I did the wilder they went.'

Unknown to Elvis, Slim Whitman had been brought to the wings by the the wild audience reaction. 'You know,' Slim remarked to one of his band, 'if that young man keeps going like that, he's going to make it real big one of these days.'

Another taking part in the show was also struck by the force of the Elvis stage performance. Webb Pierce was due to go on between Elvis and Slim. He shook his head in bewilderment and quietly walked off without even attempting a performance.

One month later, Sam Phillips decided it was time for a second single. The lead song was to be *Good Rockin' Tonight*, with *I Don't Care if the Sun Don't Shine* on the B side. The single was released on 25 September and one week later Elvis appeared on stage at the Grand Ole Opry for a live radio broadcast. It looked as if Elvis was about to break into the big time. The Grand Ole Opry was, and remains, one of the most powerful venues in American music.

A relaxed Elvis at Christmas. One of his earliest theme albums was the classic *Elvis Christmas Album* of 1957. This was only his fifth album but was already in the forefront of developments in music as the idea of an album as a collection of singles was abandoned in favour of one which was a cohesive whole.

Into the Limelight

The Great Elvis Sneer. A characteristic of Elvis from his earliest days, the sneer was later developed to become almost a trademark. During his great TV comeback show, Elvis joked about it saying, 'I did 29 movies like that.'

Live radio shows began to be broadcast in the 1920s, with local country music talent being the prime product. The show gave time to new talent, and showcased the greatest stars on the circuit. To gain such a prestigious radio slot with just two singles was an impressive achievement.

For this vital performance, the band decided on the gentle *Blue Moon of Kentucky* followed by their hit single, *That's All Right*. It proved to be a disastrous choice. The first song went down well enough, but *That's All Right* was met by only polite applause. The audience of the Grand Ole Opry was made up of the country music establishment and liked its music to be just that – country. The heavy influences of gospel and blues in the Elvis songs was just not appreciated.

Jim Denny, the manager of the Grand Ole Opry, greeted Elvis as he came off stage with the words, 'Listen boy, you should quit singing and go back to driving a truck.' Elvis, already dismayed by the poor audience response, was devastated. It was the lowest point Elvis was to know for many years. Moreover, the new single was not selling well in the stores – it did not even reach the top 30. More ominously, the hit – *That's All Right* – had failed to break out of the Deep South onto the national stage. The dynamic new sound was written off as some freak type of black music in the Northern states and was thought too provincial in the West.

Faced with such discouragement, Elvis seriously considered giving up music and concentrating his efforts on his night classes. But Scotty Moore persuaded Elvis to give it one more try with the next radio show for which they already had a booking.

The next show was the Louisiana Hayride, broadcast live from a theatre in Shreveport, Louisiana, and due just two weeks later. Although the Louisiana Hayride consciously modelled itself on the Grand Ole Opry, it was a different type of show. The audience was younger and less attached to traditional country music. It was, in short, just the audience for

Elvis. As before, the band played *Blue Moon of Kentucky* and *That's All Right* and this time the audience reacted as Elvis had hoped. The younger fans were overwhelmingly enthusiastic and ecstatic phone calls soon proved that the radio audience had loved Elvis as well.

The Louisiana Hayride at once offered the band the chance to play regularly for $42 a time. It wasn't much, but it was enough. Elvis handed in his notice to his employer and left night school. Still performing as Hillbilly Cat and the Blue Moon Boys, the band got in touch with DJ Bob Neal, who had extensive contacts in the live music business. They struck a deal in which Neal was to organize live appearances by the band in which Neal was to take a cut of 15

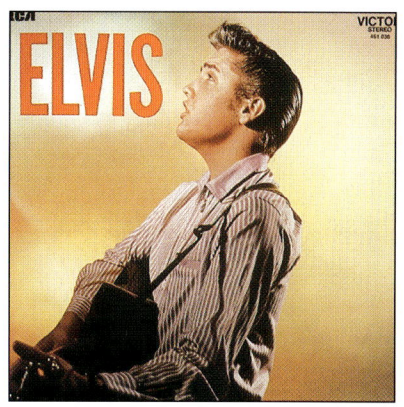

LEFT
An early publicity shot of Elvis. As with other stars of the time, Elvis was expected to adopt a variety of poses to appeal to different markets and audiences.

Into the Limelight

As an accomplished guitarist himself, Elvis frequently accompanied himself in the early days. Among the most treasured memories of his early fans were the times they were able to approach him for photo opportunities. Elvis was unfailingly polite and considerate on such occasions, though his later fame caused such opportunities to became rarer.

per cent, which was fairly modest by the standards of managers at the time. Of the remainder, Elvis got half while Scotty and Bill split the rest between them. Soon the band was visiting all sorts of venues across the Southern states. Bars, theatres, county fairs and parties all benefited from the Elvis stage magic.

At the same time, the young singer was building up a distinct youth following. The key to this almost fanatical devotion was to be found in Elvis himself and his amazing stage persona. The flashy, almost outrageous clothing was not just meant for the stage. Elvis wore such outfits every day of his life, as Scotty Moore's wife could testify. But on the stage they assumed an added dimension, distinguishing him from any other performer.

Elvis's good looks also played a part in his appeal. That he was good-looking cannot be denied, nor can the fact that he was far from handsome in the conventional, movie-star way. Early fans remarked on his great, rather sad grey eyes, later to be emphasized with stage makeup. The vulnerability present in the eyes was, however, belied by natural good manners and respect for his elders. But both qualities were contradicted by the famous Elvis sneer, at times suggestive of contempt, at others of a cynical response to what was going on around him. Even his good natured smile could deteriorate into a curled lip on occasion, which is not to say that Elvis was ever cynical about the music world or his own success. More likely it was a manifestation of surprise at the change in his fortunes.

But the main impact of Elvis's stage performance was what Scotty Moore called 'the wiggle'. It was his extraordinary gyrations

which caused him to be dubbed Elvis the Pelvis, a term of abuse which stuck and later came to be regarded as a term of endearment. It is difficult for us, after exposure to years of pop shows full of dancing and physical mobility to realize just how astonishing Elvis was when he first appeared on stage. Until that time singers were expected to be quite static. Stars such as Bing Crosby stood in front of a microphone and just sang. They only made slight arm movements, aimed at indicating or emphasizing emotion, but which could hardly be regarded as movements, as performed by Elvis. Even a raised eyebrow was thought to be enough to get a song across to an attentive audience. This was due to the classical training of singers of the day, but technology also played a part.

The microphones of the 1940s were large, heavy but delicate. Any singer who picked one up on stage would be likely to find that the thin carbon membrane had broken. And if he moved around his voice would quickly fade, the microphone having difficulty picking up any sound more than a few inches away. By the time Elvis came along, things had changed. Microphones were more robust and could put up with a great deal of rough treatment which would have been impossible earlier on. One of the earliest photographs of Elvis on stage, at the Louisiana Hayride of October 1954, clearly shows his technique. To emphasize a moment of intimacy in the song, Elvis is shown pulling the microphone back so that the stand is at an angle of around 60 degrees. Another shows him at the end of his act, face down on the stage gasping the last few phrases of a lyric into a microphone laid flat down on the stage before him. Coming from a tradition where movement was a part of singing, Elvis saw no reason why he should not make the microphone part of his performance, and technology had reached a point that allowed him to do just that.

His extraordinary gyrations were, to him, just a part of his music. But others disagreed. His swaying hips and convulsive jerks were thought by some to have sexual connotations. When Elvis hit the national stage, he was denounced by church leaders, politicians and others concerned at the impact rock and roll, and Elvis in particular, was having on the youth of America. At one point a reporter asked Elvis if he knew what he was doing on stage or if his movements were unconscious. Entirely missing the loaded sexual content of the question, Elvis answered simply. 'Unconscious? No, sir. I know what I'm doing. I'm dancing.'

Years later, Elvis may have gyrated for more obviously provocative reasons, but at this stage in his life there seems no reason to doubt his own view that he was merely dancing.

The raw energy of Elvis on stage, and the emotion it inspired in younger fans, also sprang from other influences. America was enjoying an economic boom after a time of brutal war. Enormous optimism was spreading across the whole of America, felt even more strongly by the young than other sections of society. All that many of Elvis's teenage fans had ever known was healthy living, stability and peace and good job prospects for the future. And the very concept of being a 'teenager' was just beginning to take hold. Until then, children had been given a basic education before going out to work aged 12 or 14. They went directly from being children to young adults, with no period of transition, expected to take their place in the world of work. Only the very wealthy stayed on to go to college.

But by the mid-1950s all this was changing. Less wealthy children were staying on at high school until they were 17 or 18. Although still in full-time education, they took part-time jobs and as a result had disposable income to spend. The new teenager had money, but none of the responsibility that went with being an adult. It was a strange new twist of life, and the new youth were desperate for role models and icons. For a great many, it was Elvis on stage with whom teenagers identified. He was young, good-looking, talented, and entirely uninhibited. No wonder the young audiences of the Southern states went wild for Elvis and his band.

One female fan recalled the excitement

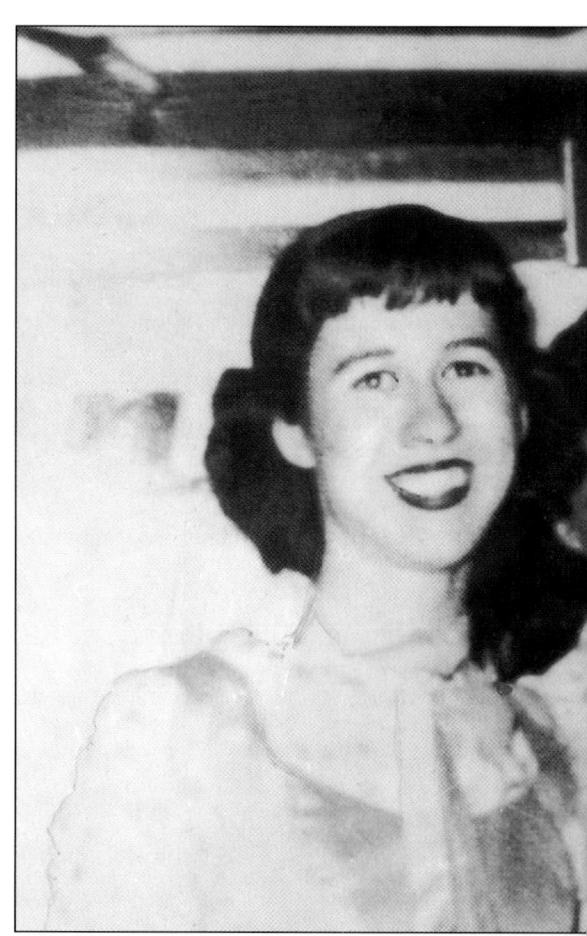

among young Elvis fans at the time. *'I was 11 years old. Some of my older friends figured that Elvis would have to travel through our town, Calvert, to get from Waco to Houston* [two venues he was playing in December 1954]. *They planned to wait downtown all night to see him. My mother wouldn't let me go, saying they would never see Elvis, but my mother was wrong this time. They spotted Elvis's car sometime after midnight and chased it to Hearne, 7 miles away. Elvis and his group were travelling in only one car then. They stopped at a gas station. His group was not very courteous, but Elvis was very mannerly. He let them take his picture, sang part of a song for them, gave away his comb, signed autographs and made life-long fans. One of my friends got his autograph for me and another sold copies of the pictures she took. I still have the black-and-white photograph, but have lost the autograph over the years. I still regret not getting to be there that wonderful night when Calvert kids got to meet Elvis.'*

Encouraged by the growing number of fans, and by the Louisiana Hayride contract, Elvis went back to recording. On 10 December 1954 he returned to the Sun studios with Scotty and Bill to cut a new single. The A side, *Milkcow Boogie*, has not entered into the company of classic Elvis tracks, which in some ways is surprising as it was the first time Elvis used techniques which would remain with him throughout his career. The song had been written as a rhythm and blues number in 1935, and it was in this style that the song begins. After a few bars, however, Elvis breaks in to stop the music. 'Hold it, fellas,' he says. 'That don't move me. Let's get real, real gone.' At

Elvis poses with a trio of young fans after a stage show. Part of his phenomenal success in the Southern states was due to his welcoming and humble attitude towards people who admired him. It seemed that he was always slightly surprised to find people so keen to meet him. His fans remarked how different Elvis was from other stars.

Into the Limelight

once the boys pick the tune up again, but this time in a fast rock style which was coming to be regarded as the Elvis sound. This trick of breaking into a song to make a comment or to change the beat was to feature in several later recordings and stage shows.

The disc was released, the artists credited by name as Elvis Presley with Scotty and Bill, the old 'Hillbilly Cat' tag having been dropped. This was odd, as the band had acquired a fourth member, the bass of Bill Black being no longer enough to give the music its urgent beat. Johnny Bernero was brought in by Sam Phillips to play drums and it was an inspired decision. The insistent drum-beat was exactly what was required in the developing style of rock and roll. Within a few weeks, Bernero was replaced with D.J. Fontana for live performances. Fontana immediately picked up the new type of rock and roll Elvis was creating and stuck with the star.

But Elvis was not neglecting his roots. The session also included two country numbers, *You're a Heartbreaker*, which was released as the B side of the new single and, *You're Right, I'm Left, She's Gone*, which was not released for over three years.

The new single did not do particularly well, failing to make it nation-wide. Another session in January produced two good rock numbers, *Mystery Train* and *Baby Let's Play House*, though they were not released. However, Elvis was not depressed. Demands for live appearances continued to flood in as Bob Neal did his job well. By this time, Elvis could command $400 for a show, earning more money than he had ever thought possible. But

Elvis poses outside his parents' house, 1034 Audubon Drive in Memphis, with some of the fans who habitually visited it, hoping to catch a glimpse of their hero. The neighbours continually complained about the crowds of teenagers hanging around.

Bob Neal had even bigger ideas.

In May, Bob Neal managed to book Elvis and the band on a major tour, the Hank Snow Jamboree. This tour was a major break for any artist aiming at a career in live performance and Elvis was thrilled. His elation was also due to another reason, however, for Hank Snow was one of Elvis's idols from his youth. This top country artist was much admired by Elvis, and has remained a giant of country music. Also on the tour was Slim Whitman, whom Elvis had earlier supported and who had been quick to spot Elvis's talents.

The tour proved to be a good earner for Elvis in more ways than one. In addition to his fee for appearing, Elvis received a boost to his recording income. Wherever the tour played, demand for the *Milkcow Boogie* single accelerated. The teenagers who saw Elvis on stage clamoured for his records. In response, Sam Phillips hurriedly released *Baby Let's Play House*, backed by *You're Right, I'm Left, She's Gone*. For some unexplained reason, however, the B side was entitled, *I'm Left, You're Right, She's Gone*. This is neither what Elvis sings, nor does it make a great deal of sense. But the title stuck and is still used on compilation albums released decades later.

In July, as the tour ended, Sam Phillips decided to release *Mystery Train*, but did not have a suitable backing track. Back to the recording studios went Elvis and his band and three songs were recorded: *I Forgot to Remember to Forget Her*, *Trying to Get to You* and *Tomorrow Night*. Without doubt *I Forgot to Remember to Forget Her* was the best track and was used as the B side to *Mystery Train*. As with all the Sun singles, this used the format of rock and roll on the A side and country on the B side. There was, as yet, no rock singles charts and all the Elvis songs appeared on the country charts. *Mystery Train* reached the number 11 slot on the Billboard Country Chart, restoring his ranking as a recording artist.

Though nobody could know it at the time, this was to be the last Sun recording by Elvis. The Hank Snow Jamboree had working for it one of the most flamboyant publicists in the music business: Colonel Tom Parker. He soon spotted Elvis as a major talent and decided to take the boy on. The partnership was to last until Elvis's death.

OPPOSITE
A sultry Elvis in an early publicity shot. The horseshoe ring caused a rush of anxiety among his younger female fans when the rumour spread that it was given to Elvis by a girlfriend. Elvis quickly scotched the idea in a television interview.

CHAPTER THREE
THE PELVIS

OPPOSITE
The great gold 'most famous suit in the world'. Although without doubt the most famous of the early Elvis outfits, he did not actually wear it very often. The jacket was seen more often than the trousers, and both have survived in good enough condition to be put on show at Graceland.

The partnership between Elvis and Colonel Tom Parker was to be the defining one in the career of the young rock singer; but it was not one which clicked immediately. It took hard work on the part of Colonel Parker, but he was a shrewd operator and set about his task in an efficient manner. It took several months, but eventually Parker became Elvis Presley's sole manager, and came to exert a powerful influence over the progress of the star's career.

Much has been written about Tom Parker, not all of it complimentary, and he is certainly an enigmatic figure. In part this was because he did his best to hide his true origins, causing odd and bizarre rumours to circulate about him. He was born André Cornelius van Kuijk in Breda, a town in the Netherlands. At some point in the 1920s he visited the United States and returned there in 1929 to join the army as unemployment hit Holland. The 20-year-old van Kuijk served in the 64th Coastal Battery, a unit charged with guarding harbours and coastal towns against shellfire from enemy ships. During the First World War, several British coastal towns had suffered badly at the hands of the German High Seas Fleet. American military planners were determined that the United States would not suffer a similar fate in any future war. As usual, however, the military strategists missed out on the fact that time had moved on, and disregarded the threat of bomb-carrying aircraft.

After three years in the army, van Kuijk married a girl named Mary Ross and took a job with a travelling carnival. His title 'Colonel' has nothing to do with his army service, being an honorary title granted to him by the State of Virginia some years later. By the time he started with the carnival, van Kuijk was calling himself Thomas Andrew Parker and claiming to have been born in Virginia. Although much of this phase of his life is lost in obscurity, one story persists regarding his hit show *Colonel Parker and his Dancing Chickens*. According to this, Parker ran a sideshow in which chickens danced to music from a record player. Although he claimed that the chickens had been specially trained, this was not the truth. In fact the sand in which the chickens danced was laid on a metal plate heated from below by gas flames. The only reason the chickens danced when Parker turned on the music was that he also turned up the gas at the same time.

The Pelvis

Whatever the truth of the dancing chickens and other stories, Parker clearly did not waste his time travelling with the carnival. He learned many publicity tricks, and invented others which he eagerly tried out on the punters he attracted to his shows. By the end of the 1930s, Parker had risen from running sideshows to becoming a full-time publicist and promoter. In 1942 he was hired by country music star Eddy Arnold; this was Parker's first taste of the music business and he must have liked it, for he never left it. Having taken Arnold to the top as far as country music was concerned, Parker took on Hank Snow. It was as publicist for Hank Snow's tour that he met Presley.

At the time of their meeting, the young singer had a contract with Bob Neal which still had some months to run. It was also clear that

Elvis answers questions at a press conference. From his very first interview on the local Memphis radio station, WHBQ, Elvis was wary of revealing his personal life to public gaze. But he knew his fans deserved to learn more about their hero and underwent this ordeal whenever asked to do so.

Presley and his band owed a great deal to Neal and had no intention of running out on him. However, Parker knew that Neal had his hands full with his various commitments in the music business. He also quickly realized that Elvis was very much a home body, and extremely devoted to his family.

Using his position as tour publicist, Parker began to find reasons for visiting Elvis at home. Whenever he called by, Parker made a point of chatting to Vernon and to Gladys about how well their son was doing on the road. Before long he was emphasizing to Vernon just how much fame and money could come Elvis's way as long as he had the right type of manager. He warned that a young boy needed protection from more predatory executives and the fast women abundant in the music industry. Colonel Parker's argument was helped by the fact that what he said held more than an element of truth. Moreover, he had a good reputation for keeping a close eye on his clients.

Only when he was certain that the Presley parents would accept him did Parker turn to Elvis and to Bob Neal, offering to handle the promotional side of a few concerts Neal had arranged for Elvis and the band. So successful was Parker that, a month later, Presley signed up with him. The contract with Neal still had some time to run, but he seems to have been happy to take a back seat; after all, he was now being paid for doing very little indeed. Parker, for his part, was to take 25 per cent of everything Elvis made. The new deal was set for success. As Parker once told Elvis, 'You stay young and sexy and I'll make us both rich as rajahs.'

But before Elvis was really able to hit the big time, Colonel Parker had to tie up one other loose end: Sam Phillips and Sun Records. As Phillips would have been the first to admit, his was a local recording company catering for Southern tastes. He had neither the resources nor the contacts to handle a star as big as the

ABOVE LEFT
Gladys Presley had a pet dog which was very much part of the family in Elvis's childhood. He never entirely lost his love of animals, though this did not become apparent to the public until the release of the movie *G.I. Blues*.

ABOVE
Elvis talks to the audience in a Southern school hall while his backing band prepares for the next number.

The Pelvis

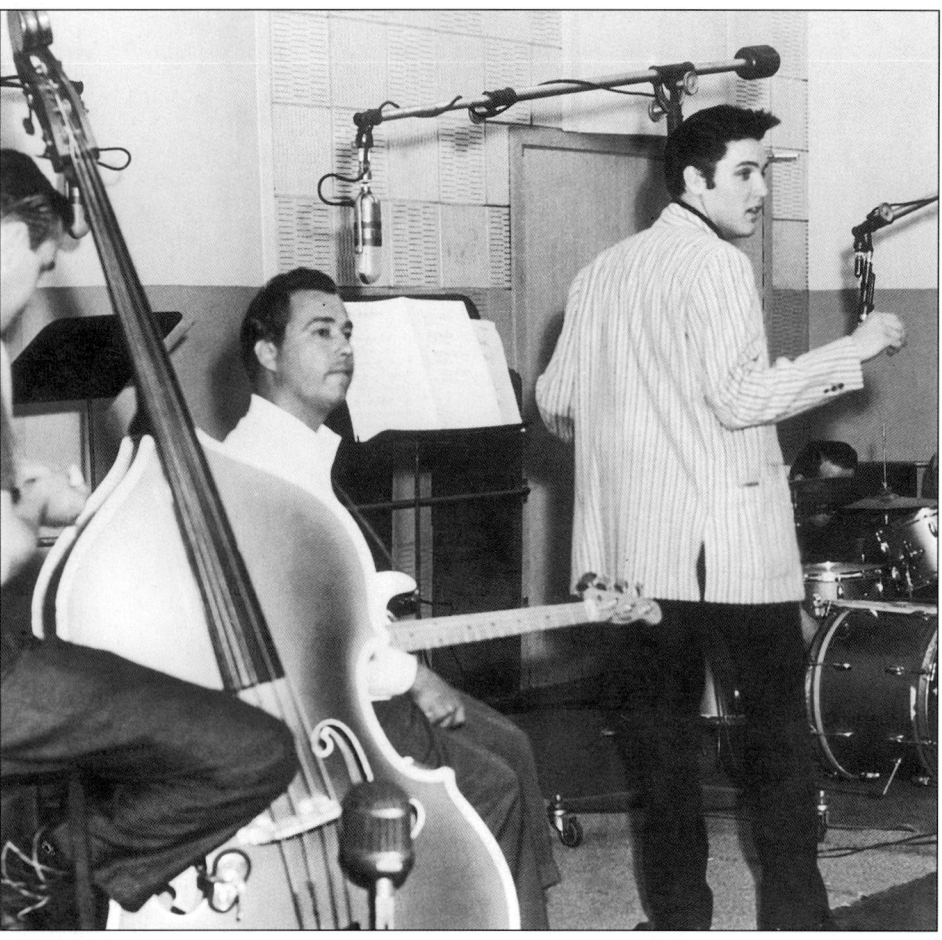

Elvis in the studio with Scotty Moore at one of the earlier RCA sessions. The bass in the foreground is probably being played by Bill Black. Elvis wears one of his favourite pink-and-black outfits.

Colonel intended Elvis to be. Elvis had to sign with a major record company, and that meant leaving Sun. The Colonel was determined that any major label deal Elvis committed himself to signing would include provision for Sun and Sam Phillips. In the event, all the Sun recordings, whether released or not, were bought out for several thousand dollars, and Sun was allowed to sell its remaining stock for its own profit on the back of new publicity. Sam Phillips accepted the deal and never complained about it after Elvis became a major star.

In fact both Sam Phillips and Bob Neal benefited indirectly from their days with Elvis. As soon as Elvis hit the big time the two men set up Stars Inc., a music management team. Capitalizing on their reputation for having 'found' Elvis, the men attracted a whole stable of young talent, including such great names as Jerry Lee Lewis, Carl Perkins and Roy Orbison.

The Colonel, meanwhile, was putting together a record deal which would be the foundation of Elvis's future greatness. At the time there were three major record labels: RCA Victor, Columbia-CBS and Atlantic. Columbia bid first, offering $15,000. However, it viewed Elvis as a talented country singer and the company was known to have a bias against the rougher end of the rock market. Atlantic made a firm bid next, offering $25,000 up front, but the Colonel was uncertain that the company understood the type of publicity needed.

In the event it was RCA Victor which Colonel Parker accepted. It helped that two stars previously managed by the Colonel were already at RCA Victor. Hank Snow and Eddy Arnold had no complaints about the way they were being treated, nor about the financial deals RCA Victor handled. The deal was finalized on 20 November 1955. RCA paid $25,000, plus a $5,000 cash payment to Elvis himself. It was with this money that Elvis made perhaps his most famous purchase. 'I went out and bought Momma a pink Cadillac.' This perfectly encapsulates every aspect of Elvis's character. He was generous to a fault, devoted to his mother, obsessed with motor cars and instantly drawn to anything flashy – the flashier the better. Although other cars came and went, the pink Crown Victoria Cadillac remained and is still part of the Presley estate.

Within weeks, RCA Victor had its new artist in the recording studio. Not only was the technical equipment at RCA's Nashville studio far superior to anything at Sun Records, but the company could afford top quality back-up. In addition to Elvis, Scotty Moore, Bill Black and D.J. Fontana, the company laid on guitarist Chet Atkins, pianist Floyd Cramer and a trio of backing singers. It took some time for the new arrivals to settle in with those who knew how Elvis worked, but the end result was well worthwhile.

The first number recorded was *I Got a Woman*, a fast rock number. Although more than competent, there is, however, something of the Elvis dynamism missing. Perhaps the musicians were trying so hard to work well together that spontaneity was lost in the process. Two slow songs came next: *I'm Counting on You* and *I Was the One*. By the time the group got to the fourth song they were gelling well together and the track became perhaps the first and greatest of the Elvis classics.

Heartbreak Hotel captures the raw energy of the Elvis sound developed at Sun and on the road in the Southern states, but with a bigger sound provided by the musicians of RCA Victor. This was the defining track for Elvis, the moment his skills and energy were honed to a professional edge which made him the King. For many fans this single track says it all.

Chet Atkins, later to become a legendary figure in country music, said, 'Elvis was electrifying. He was so different in everything he did. He dressed differently and moved differently from anybody we had ever seen.' It was Chet who persuaded Elvis to record some of the vocals on a concrete staircase at the back

TOP

Elvis being escorted by police. As his fame grew, Elvis became accustomed to being guided through crowds of screaming fans; but the police formed a less welcome escort after his arrest for assaulting a gas station attendant. Elvis was later acquitted of all charges.

The Pelvis

OPPOSITE

Elvis relaxes with Colonel Tom Parker (in striped shirt) and business executives. The Colonel handled all Elvis's business affairs as his manager, the extent of his power being the subject of much debate. It is clear, however, that Elvis was happy to go along with most of Parker's decisions.

of the RCA Victor studios. The result was a slight echo which emphasized the loneliness of the song. It is said that Colonel Parker disliked the 'stairwell sound', but was overruled and these were the vocals used on the final record.

Backed by *I Was the One*, *Heartbreak Hotel* was released on 27 January 1956. In just over 60 days it was number 1 on the Billboard Popular Music Chart, the Country Music Chart and the Rhythm and Blues Chart. No other disc had ever achieved as much and it marked Elvis as a performer going places.

The day after the single was released, Elvis hit national television. The variety show, the *Tommy and Jimmy Dorsey Show*, was losing in a ratings war with the *Perry Como Show*, ironically a major RCA success. In the hope of attracting a younger audience, the veteran Dorsey brothers sidestepped their big band background to book Presley, Colonel Parker persuading them to part with $1,250 for that first show. The hoped-for younger audience turned out in strength as soon as it was known that Elvis would be on stage. As usual Elvis made quite an impact with his appearance; knowing black-and-white television would fail to do justice to colour, Elvis appeared in black trousers and shirt with a white tie. When the band started with *Shake, Rattle and Roll*, the teenagers began to cheer, but when Elvis began to dance they went wild.

Jackie Gleason, the producer, at once booked Elvis for five more shows. But even as he signed Presley up, Gleason was telling his colleagues, 'He can't last. I tell you flat. He can't last.' It was a view held by many at the time: rock and roll was a new phenomenon –

associated as much with juvenile delinquency and gang fights as with music. Cinemas brave enough to show rock and roll movies had to remove their plush cushions and curtains or risk having them destroyed. Because the musicians involved were, like Elvis, largely young and poor, the music establishment refused to take them seriously and rock and roll was seen by the majority as a violent, unwelcome phenomenon and, hopefully, a flash in the pan.

To some extent Colonel Tom Parker and Elvis himself shared this view. Elvis did not rate himself too highly as a musician. 'If I stop moving, they'll stop coming,' he said of his fans at about this time. Both he and Parker seem to have considered themselves supremely lucky to have been in the right place at the right time and the Colonel at least was determined to make as much money as possible before the rock and roll bubble burst and Elvis ceased to be fashionable.

It was this short-term view that led to the Colonel making one of his most counter-productive business deals. He set up two music publishing companies called Elvis Presley Music and Gladys Music to produce sheet music for the arrangements and songs made famous by Elvis. The complex contracts these companies had entered into with RCA Victor and songwriters meant that a sizable chunk of the royalties were siphoned off from the songwriters and given to Elvis instead. Many of the established songwriters objected strongly and refused either to write for Elvis or to let him record their songs. Although it gave an instant boost to the Elvis cash flow, the long-term effect was to deprive Elvis of some of the

The Pelvis

best rock and roll songs of the era.

At the time, however, there were no such doubts. After the Dorsey show, Elvis travelled to New York to record at the main RCA Victor studio. Elvis had his three original backers, but Chet Atkins and the other RCA Nashville stars were missing, replaced by other RCA musicians. Again, the new team got together quickly and established such classics as *Blue Suede Shoes*, *My Baby Left Me* and *Shake Rattle and Roll*.

Meanwhile, Presley was continuing to play live shows and, on 3 April, returned to television. Again the Colonel booked Presley onto a show which was slipping in its ratings and therefore desperate to obtain a guaranteed audience. The *Milton Berle Show* agreed to pay an unheard of sum of $10,000 for a two-show deal. The first show went out on 3 April 1956 from the USS *Hancock*, Elvis appearing totally in black, apart from a bright pink tie. His set included *Heartbreak Hotel* and *Blue Suede Shoes*. His performance was rather restrained by his own standards, and it was clear the audience was not quite certain how to take it. The few gyrations he worked into the act were greeted with murmurs of disapproval as much as by shouts and cheers.

Three weeks later, Elvis Presley was booked into Las Vegas, the premier live venue for American performers. For once the Colonel had made a bad decision. The Vegas audience was older and more staid than most, with not a teenager in sight. Elvis played for only a week before his contract was broken by mutual consent, the Vegas hotel hired a safe comedian, and Presley went back to his adoring teenage fans.

The second *Milton Berle Show* on 5 June caused real trouble. As a finale, Elvis performed *Hound Dog*, soon to be released as a single. As the song reached its climax, Elvis grabbed the microphone and undulated around the stage in a manner so fluid, dynamic and overtly sexy that it surpassed anything he had even done on film. There is a brief shot of the television audience where faces register emotions ranging from admiration and wonder in the younger viewers, to surprise and shock in older ones. When Elvis finished, Milton Berle came out to engage the audience in some good natured joshing. He even made a parody of the singer's movements by swinging his hips and shaking his legs. The band cut in with a few bars, and Elvis joined in. But unknown to Elvis or Berle, the damage had been done.

Vast numbers of parents were watching the show to have a look at this Elvis their kids seemed so keen on and they did not like what they saw. Over 700,000 letters of complaint flooded in to Milton Berle. 'Uncle Miltie' had

Elvis about to be presented with an award. As his fame spread, Elvis's reputation fluctuated – at times he was regarded as a teenage rebel, at others as a clean-cut young man. Some organizations made awards to Elvis, other heaped abuse upon him.

thrown away his reputation for providing wholesome family entertainment. The suggestive movements were too much for Middle America and Elvis was plunged into a sea of controversy. Matters deteriorated when a gas station attendant, in a fracas over what was claimed to be good-natured banter, accused Elvis of punching him. Elvis was eventually cleared, but there was no doubt in anyone's mind that he was the dangerous face of the sinister rock and roll phenomenon.

A few days after the Berle sensation, Elvis appeared on stage at the Sam Houston Coliseum in Houston, Texas. The local newspaper sent along one of its more senior reporters, Dick de Pugh, to see what the fuss was all about.

'The wails and screams of more than 8,000 rock 'n' roll idolizers gave a tumultuous opening to the first show of the famed Tennessee playboy, Elvis Presley, Saturday. The howling "hound dog" artist with the rhythmic accomplices were met with mob hysteria to open their two-performance stand here.

'Presley's appearance was preceded by six variety acts to warm up the crowd into a frenzy. The circus prelude included one torch singer, two acrobatic acts, a comedian, a slack wire act and a quartet. Swept in the [entrance] of the Coliseum by a police guard, the greasy, side-burned hillbilly took to the stage an hour later. Screams and lamentations kept up without relief for four minutes and 50 seconds. He entered the arena like a wild calf and began his bellowing to the tune of his million seller Heartbreak Hotel. *All that was heard of this number was the title. Screams from the crowd drowned out any other sound Presley could produce. Three times he paused his panorama of bump and grind to plead with the audience to listen to him. Deafening roars were the answers each time.*

'In the midst of the teenage tumult, a squad of 50 police officers, emergency corpsmen and firemen were circulating the aisles to keep admirers from rushing the bandstand. Elvis rolled and wiggled through Blue Suede Shoes, *adding his hippy oomph to an agonizing rendition of* Love Me, *and pulsated vigorously as he groaned though* Long Tall Sally. *Holding his hands to his ears so he could hear himself, he wore a guitar slung around his neck, seldom striking a chord. He rocked on his toes, pointed to the kids in the auditorium and sang to them and made a quick exit on a little number called* Hound Dog.

'Toward the end of Elvis's second show on Saturday night, a hysterical teen-ager with flowing ponytail broke through the police line surrounding the stage and rushed her idol. Police carried her back to her seat, but she had broken the ice. Teen-age girls en masse clamored for Presley, and rushed the stage until the singer was s whisked off in a waiting police car to his suite at the Shamrock Hilton Hotel.

'Statistics: No one fainted and no one injured.'

There could be no doubt that Elvis was a major star, with all that that entailed. By the autumn, Colonel Parker was able to joke, 'When I met Elvis he was a kid with a million-dollar talent. Now he's a kid with a million dollars.' But the constant media exposure and reaction of hysterical fans made it impossible for Presley to

Elvis poses with a child and teddy bear to emphasize his devotion to the concept of the family. The red-and-white outfit in which Elvis sang the song *Teddy Bear* in the movie *Loving You* became a classic and quickly became one of the recognized Elvis styles.

The Pelvis

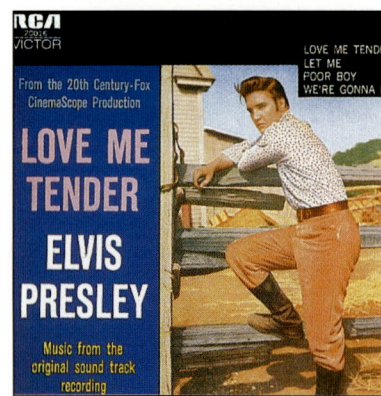

lead a normal life. He had always loved the movies but could no longer go to a regular show without being mobbed. He had to persuade cinema owners in towns where he was on tour to put on special late-night shows just for him. When not on tour he lived with his parents, but that soon became impossible when fans began to hang around the house. While Elvis was only too happy to chat to fans, his parents objected when they peered through windows and climbed into the back yard. In May the family moved to a new house in a smart area of town. His mother upset the neighbours when she realized that the garden was big enough to keep chickens, something she had always missed in the city.

In July 1956, Elvis was booked to appear on the *Steve Allen Show*. While Steve Allen and his producers needed the boost to ratings Elvis could guarantee, they had no wish to attract the bad publicity which had hit Milton Berle so hard. At the start of the show, Steve Allen went on screen to emphasize: 'We want to do a show the whole family can watch and enjoy, and we always do.' When Elvis appeared he was dressed in white tie and tails, like a modern-day Fred Astaire. There the resemblance ended when Elvis pulsated his way through his latest hit, *I Want You, I Need You, I Love You*. Then, when Steve Allen brought on a droopy hound dog, even Elvis could manage little in the way of showmanship as he sang *Hound Dog*. In a sketch later in the show, Elvis was the butt of several jokes concerning poor white Southerners. If Steve Allen avoided upsetting Middle America, he certainly upset the Elvis fans. Thousands of letters poured in objecting to the way Elvis had been treated.

The next major television appearance came on 9 September when Elvis appeared on the *Ed Sullivan Show*. This time, Colonel Parker managed to get $50,000, breaking his own record for obtaining television fees. The show broke all records for ratings when about 50 million people, some 82 per cent of all television-watching Americans, tuned in to see Elvis rock through *Don't Be Cruel*, *Hound Dog* and *Love Me Tender*. A second appearance came on 28 October, but it was the show of 6 January 1957 which again caused controversy.

Not only were letters of complaint pouring in, but newspapers were stirring up feeling against Elvis and his suggestive hip movements; the producers decided that Elvis could only be shown from the waist up. If this was designed to put a stop to the controversy, it backfired badly. Elvis threw himself into the act with his usual vigour, and the studio audience went wild. At home, viewers could only imagine what was going on, and what they imagined was more lurid than the reality. To make matters worse, Elvis decided that if the way his body was moving to the music could not be shown, he would compensate with his arms. It was the first appearance of the wiggling hands and waving arms which Elvis later turned into an art form of his own.

Ed Sullivan himself, however, had been so struck by Elvis the person that he placed his own reputation on the line at the end of this final show. On screen, Sullivan declared: '*I wanted to say to Elvis Presley and the country that this is a real decent fine boy, and we've never had a pleasanter experience on our show with a big name than we've had with him. You're thoroughly all right.'* These comments meant a lot to Elvis as they did much to counter the bad image of himself and his music held by many American parents.

The final Ed Sullivan show marked the high point of Elvis's career as a stage performer. He was reaching out to audiences of unprecedented size, could command almost any venue he desired, and had honed his stage show to the level of a masterpiece. But already the pressures which were to take Presley off the stage were beginning to show themselves.

Elvis and Colonel Tom Parker comparing notes about future engagements. Elvis was the most famous of Parker's artists and soon came to absorb all the Colonel's energies. Among the other stars previously handled by Parker was the country star Eddy Arnold.

CHAPTER FOUR
HITTING THE BIG TIME

The crowd goes wild as Elvis throws himself into another of his great performances. Once carried away, Elvis was capable of the most amazing gyrations, even to the extent of ending up face down on the stage, hugging the microphone.

In the spring of 1956, Colonel Tom Parker had begun spreading the word among movie journalists that Elvis was considering doing a movie, but was waiting for the right script. He even placed advertisements in the trade papers; but the breakthrough into movies came about by chance, stemming from the otherwise disastrous gigs in Las Vegas.

In the audience at a Las Vegas show was the veteran movie producer Hal Wallis. It is not known what Wallis himself thought of Elvis, but he clearly understood that if the Elvis phenomenon could be captured by Hollywood, a mint could be made from the teenage market. He contacted Colonel Parker and Elvis flew to Hollywood.

When one considers the long succession of Presley movies, it is hardly surprising that his earliest Hollywood experiences should have become the stuff of myth and legend. There was disagreement about whether or not Elvis should sing; whether or not he was being tested as a musical star or for straight acting ability. In the event, the surviving test footage shows Elvis coming onto a sound stage, backed by a curtain, with an old guitar strung around his neck. After standing for a moment, he is evidently given a signal and throws himself into *Blue Suede Shoes*. Only after a few lines does it become obvious that Elvis is miming and that his guitar has no strings.

The test was good enough: Paramount Pictures signed him up for a three-movie deal. He was to be paid $100,000 for the first film, $150,000 for the second and $200,000 for the third, assuming all three were made. Earmarked at first to play a retarded teenager with Burt Lancaster in *Rainmaker*, Elvis was pulled out and loaned to 20th Century Fox for a Western called *The Reno Brothers*.

Shooting of the film began in late August and continued until October. The stars of the picture, Richard Egan and Debra Paget, feared at first that the young teen idol would be difficult to work with, or worse still, without talent. In the event, neither was true. Elvis was always punctual and word perfect with his lines. He took acting very seriously and spent long hours in rehearsal. Elvis was determined to prove he could act.

The final movie, in which Elvis is left to run the Reno ranch in the absence of his brothers, away at the Civil War, and becomes romantically involved with fatal results, was a success. In itself a perfectly acceptable Western, the film was given a boost when the song *Love Me Tender* was released just before the movie opened. So well did the single sell that 20th Century Fox changed the title of the film also to *Love Me Tender* and hurriedly superimposed and image of Elvis singing the song over the closing scenes.

When the movie opened at the Paramount Theater in New York on 15 November 1956, a vast crowd of teenagers turned out, blocking the roads and attracting police who attempted to keep the highway open, while press photographers, hoping to catch a story, and large numbers of passersby milled about, eager to see what was going on. Public demand was so strong that Fox had to print over 500 copies of the film for distribution to movie houses at a time when 250 copies were considered adequate for feature films. In less than a week the film had turned a handsome profit; no one in Hollywood could remember such a movie and it eventually went into the top 20 most profitable films of all time. The critics panned Elvis and his acting but, Hollywood being Hollywood where money talked, nobody cared.

ABOVE

Elvis signs a movie contract with veteran producer Hal Wallis who was to oversee many of Elvis's early silver screen successes.

LEFT

In some of his early recordings, Elvis mastered the technique of slapping the rear of his guitar to help supplement the drums with a gentle echoing sound. It was a trick he used to great effect both in the studio and on stage.

Hitting the Big Time

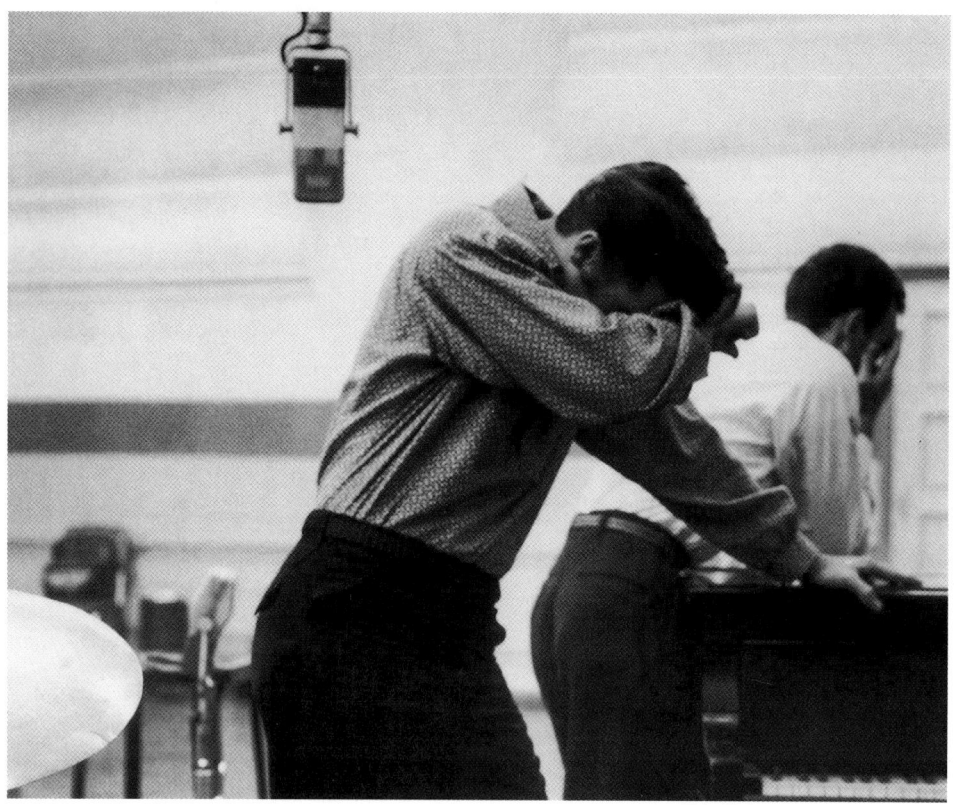

Candid shots of Elvis in his early days in the RCA studios. At that time, Elvis was spending so much time on the road performing at live concerts or preparing for television appearances that the record company was forced to use his earlier Sun recordings to augment new material.

Meanwhile, Elvis was enjoying an extended Christmas break with his family. Elvis and his parents were living at 1034 Audubon Drive, a three-bedroomed house in a rather plush neighbourhood. Many members of the extensive Presley family dropped by over Christmas, and Elvis took the opportunity to catch up with old friends, among them Sam Phillips at the old Sun studios where Elvis had cut his first discs.

Phillips managed to coax Elvis into recording songs with the new discovery Jerry Lee Lewis (who partly modelled his style on Elvis) and Carl Perkins. A young Johnny Cash was also present. Cash had travelled the country music route to fame and fortune and was an old friend of Elvis's, having on occasions appeared on stage with him, and they had also toured together before either became famous.

Because the four men were under contract to different companies, there was little chance that the recordings would be released, and Phillips may have been motivated more by a sense of fun than anything else. However, as the years passed, word of the session continued to circulate in rock and country circles and in time the recordings began to assume semi-mythical proportions. As each of the four climbed to the top of the music tree, the group became known as 'The Million Dollar Quartet'. Even though few people had heard the recordings, they were referred to in hushed tones as being the product of a group of master musicians. It was widely believed that they were of a superb, almost legendary quality.

Eventually, in 1990, the various companies involved managed to work out a publishing deal and the songs recorded in that session were released under the title *Million Dollar Quartet*. The final album contains several religious songs, including *Just a Little Talk with Jesus* and *When the Saints go Marching In*, together with such Presley rock numbers as *Don't Be*

Cruel and *Paralysed*. The album, hyped for so long, was something of a mixed bag and, perhaps inevitably, failed to quite measure up to expectations. Though there can be no doubting the musical genius of each man, their styles were too different for them to blend well together without hours of practice, and this had not happened.

Meanwhile, back in Hollywood, Paramount recognized a money-making talent when they saw one and called Elvis in to start on his first movie for them. *Loving You* was without doubt specifically intended as a vehicle for Elvis Presley's talents, and he took the starring role. His co-star was Dolores Hart, later to become a star in her own right before suddenly retiring to a convent. Elvis sung eight songs in this movie and, although the story was entirely fictitious, it revolved around a poor Southern boy who predictably finds a career as a singer. The strong similarities to Elvis Presley's own life were obvious. In the final scene, where Elvis's character performs to a packed theatre, Vernon and Gladys were part of the crowd and are clearly visible in the final shots. The main song, *Teddy Bear*, was released as a single alongside the movie and raced up the charts to the number 1 slot.

Meanwhile, Presley's increasing wealth and fame were causing great upheavals in his home life. One day, on returning home, Elvis spotted the customary crowd of fans and sightseers. Getting out of his car to sign a few autographs, Elvis was suddenly pounced upon by a group of young women who began to grab at his clothes and hair. Vernon Presley shouldered his way into the crowd together with his brother Vester and, after an unseemly scuffle, Elvis was dragged free and into the house. Clearly, this sort of thing could not be allowed to continue.

Elvis began to look around for a house with secure grounds. At the same time he turned to

Elvis seated at the piano on the Ed Sullivan Show. He liked to work out arrangements and ideas for his songs on the piano rather than the guitar. As he grew older, he also took to playing the piano for relaxation and the piano-room at Graceland was one of his favourite places.

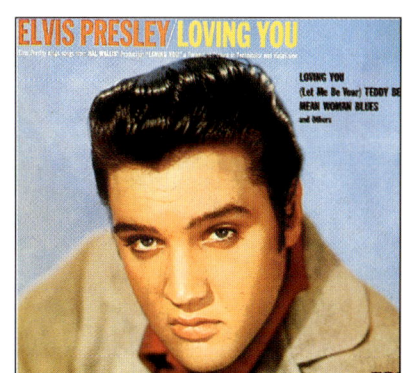

Hitting the Big Time

Red West, the school friend who had rescued him from having his head shaved some years before. While Elvis had been developing his musical career, Red had played college football and done a stint in the Marines. He eagerly accepted Elvis's offer of a job protecting him and before long had virtually moved in with the Presleys.

At about the same time, two other kids from the L. C. Humes High School were recruited by Elvis. Marty Lacker had joined the music business as a disc jockey and had kept in touch, albeit remotely, with Elvis; Marty's task was to keep everyone organized, making sure Elvis was where he was supposed to be, and on

ABOVE
Elvis photographed at the signing of his first-ever recording contract. On the left is Bob Neal, then Elvis's agent, and on the right Sam Phillips, the owner of Sun Records – the Memphis company which discovered Elvis and released his first few singles.

RIGHT
Elvis in a publicity shot at a soda fountain. Elvis's publicists tried to emphasize his boy-next-door image, though by this time he rarely attended ordinary bars due to large numbers of fans which followed him everywhere.

Elvis poses sulkily beside a giant figure of himself advertising his first appearance at Las Vegas. The event was a flop. Elvis was simply too young and brash for the older and more staid audiences of Las Vegas in the late 1950s.

Hitting the Big Time

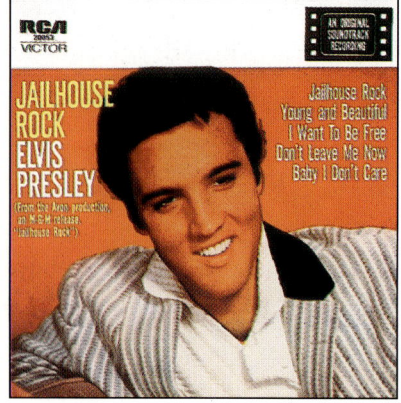

BELOW
Elvis poses with a fan during one of his seemingly endless concert tours of the early RCA days. In 1955 Elvis collapsed after a show in Jacksonville, Florida. Doctors diagnosed exhaustion and recommended total rest. The rest lasted just 2 days before Elvis was back on stage, pleasing his fans.

time, and to handle petty cash while away from home. Sonny West, Red's younger brother, was a more informal member of the group, hired merely to help out on the road. Later, however, Sonny would act as a decoy to mislead press and fans, as well as helping his brother with security. Another Memphis youth, Lamar Fike, joined the three in the Elvis entourage on the recommendation of Sam Phillips.

These four men remained close to Elvis for many years. Together they gained notoriety as 'The Memphis Mafia'. They jealously guarded Elvis from outsiders, keeping his secrets to themselves, and acted as unofficial sounding boards for Elvis's ideas and problems over the years. The name Memphis Mafia is said to have originated in the early 1960s when Elvis and his entourage were in Las Vegas on vacation. One day Elvis went to the Riviera Hotel for a business meeting where, wishing to make an impression, Elvis and the boys dressed identically in black mohair suits. As the security staff ushered them past the crowds, one onlooker asked, 'Who are these guys, the Mafia?' The remark was overheard by a news reporter and next day the term Memphis Mafia hit the news stands and remained in the public imagination.

While he was putting together a team of confidants with whom he felt comfortable, Elvis continued to look for a house. He found what he was searching for in Graceland, a 13-acre estate on the outskirts of Memphis, at Whitehaven. One of the main attractions was that the house, built in 1939, had been designed by amateur musicians to include rooms which were acoustically pure. The estate, however, dated back to the Civil War when it was named for Grace Toof, daughter of its then owner.

When Elvis, Vernon and Gladys Presley moved in, the house was a large sandstone building with an impressive colonial-style white porch surrounded by rolling gardens. Gladys was pleased to be back in a setting which was as close to the country as Memphis could offer, but for Elvis the house as it stood was only the beginning. Its 23 rooms were totally redecorated: his taste ran to the exuberant, just as it did to his clothing. Purple and gold were favourite colours, not just inside but also for the spotlights which lit up the house at night. Among other luxuries installed by Elvis were powerful air conditioning and a racquetball court.

But it was at the entrance to the estate that Elvis installed what was to become the most famous feature of the house: The Music Gate. The iron gate was designed by John Dillars working for Memphis Doors. It was constructed to be attractive and secure while offering no sharp surfaces likely to injure over-enthusiastic fans, while discretely tucked behind them was an office for the security men who guarded the entrance.

Each of the twin gates features the sweeping outline of a guitar-playing Elvis, together with musical notations, and this has become the enduring symbol of Graceland. So firmly was it identified with Elvis, that Memphis later officially redesignated the road on which it stands Elvis Presley Boulevard, Graceland becoming number 3764. The property became an extension of Elvis and his personality and over the years that it was home to the singer and his family, was altered many times.

The movie *Loving You* opened to massed crowds on 9 July 1957 in Memphis, Tennessee. Elvis and his parents, by then well established in Graceland, attended the première, but Elvis was already filming his next movie. It was to prove far better and more enduring than any of his previous efforts.

Jailhouse Rock was made for MGM in a matter of weeks and was released just three months after *Loving You* reached the cinemas. The deal was a landmark for both Elvis and MGM. In addition to a hefty fee of $250,000 in advance, Elvis also received 50 per cent of the studio profits. Again Colonel Parker had struck a good deal. *Jailhouse Rock* has proved enduringly popular and money from it continues to roll in.

The film shows Elvis at his very best as a performer and includes the title track *Jailhouse Rock*, as well as *Baby I Don't Care* and *Treat Me Nice*, all well suited to the Elvis treatment and, perhaps more important, Elvis was allowed to do some of the choreography himself. The great triumph was the important jail scene in which Elvis and a group of convicts dance in and out of cells and up and down a spiral staircase. The scene has been dubbed the first promotional video because of its frequent showings as such, but in fact it was made in the long tradition of spectacular musical settings in the movies. What was different about the film

Elvis proudly shows off one of his earliest gold records. The exact sales figures for Elvis Presley records will probably never be known, but they certainly run into hundreds of millions.

Hitting the Big Time

was its raw energy and the dominating presence of Elvis.

'I wasn't really ready for that town,' said Elvis of Hollywood at this time. 'And I don't think they were ready for me.'

But although spending increasing amounts of time in Hollywood or practising his acting, Elvis had not abandoned either the stage or the recording studio. In August and September of 1956, Elvis and his regular band cut several tracks at studios in Hollywood. Among the many songs recorded was one with a special place in the Elvis legend: *Old Shep* was the song he had performed at his first public appearance and has been used several times since. Though the song has not been treated to the Presley rock and roll style, it is interesting for its place in Elvis's early development.

The next trip to the recording studio, in January 1957, brought Elvis right back to his musical roots with a pair of gospel songs. *Peace in the Valley* is one of the great classics of Southern Christian music and Elvis had included it in many performances before finally getting around to recording it. *Take My Hand, Precious Lord* was the second gospel number recorded in the same session and, alongside the sacred music, Elvis recorded a number of rock and blues numbers including *All Shook Up* and *Got a Lot of Livin' to Do*.

The following weeks saw a flurry of studio activity as Elvis embarked upon what was then a new and risky venture. It was decided to release an entire album of songs to coincide with the screening of the movie *Loving You*. It was not unknown for singles to be released from movies, but an entire collection of songs

was a new concept. Unfortunately, the movie did not include enough tracks to fill an album, so some hard work was put in to produce songs which matched those of the film.

Although the songs for the movie *Jailhouse Rock* were recorded over a few days in May, they were not released as a soundtrack album. Instead, Elvis concentrated on perhaps the most popular, the non-rock Elvis Christmas Album. The collection of songs has struck many people as odd, ranging from the rock and roll *Santa Bring My Baby Back to Me* to the classic hymn *Oh Little Town of Bethlehem* and the humorous children's classic *Here Comes Santa Claus*. Although in many ways the album does not sit together very well, it does provide a good insight into Elvis's varied styles and interests at the time. In any case, the idea of concept albums had yet to be developed.

Looking around for a role which would both stretch the talents of its young star and give the audience the music it craved, Paramount came up with the novel, *A Stone for Danny Fisher*, by Harold Robbins. The oscar-winning director Michael Curtiz, who had earlier worked with Errol Flynn and Humphrey Bogart, was hired. The title was changed to *King Creole* to emphasize its New Orleans background, and to give the film a snappier title.

Elvis plays a sombre, violent character who works in the seedy nightclubs of Bourbon Street in New Orleans. Torn between his sense of right and wrong and the brutal world in which he lives, the Danny Fisher character gave Elvis the chance to show some genuine acting ability in portraying a character completely unlike himself. That Elvis carried the part off well was mostly due to the constant encouragement of Michael Curtiz who seemed determined to turn the singer into an actor. But much credit must go to Elvis, who worked hard and readily accepted all the instructions and tips being offered to him. The co-stars Walter Matthau and Carolyn Jones were top-rate Hollywood actors who had both been nominated for Oscars, and Presley was able to learn a lot from them.

But before Elvis could begin filming he received something of a shock. At the age of 23, Elvis found himself called up before the next draft board, due on 19 December 1957, which posed immediate problems for both Elvis and the authorities. Elvis was under contract to film *King Creole*, pre-production of which was complete, as well as scheduled to produce a soundtrack album. The board, meanwhile, found itself bombarded with criticism from teenage and even older fans, claiming that the draft was a deep laid government plot to sabotage Elvis and the rock and roll phenomenon.

Fortunately for all concerned, U.S. conscription rules allow draft boards to grant deferment of induction on various grounds. Elvis applied for 60 days reprieve because of his movie contract, and this was at once granted. Elvis headed for Hollywood to cut the album and shoot the movie before, on 24 March 1958, being inducted into the U.S. Army.

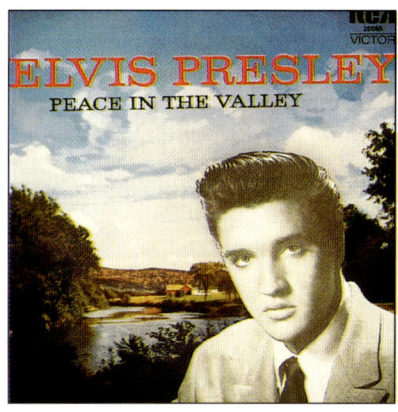

BELOW
Elvis and one of his beloved Cadillacs. 'When I was a kid,' Elvis later recalled, 'I'd sit out on the porch and watch those long, low cars whiz by. I told myself, one of these days, when I'll be all growed up, I'm gonna have two Cadillacs sittin' out front of our place, one for my folks and one for me. Now I done better than that.'

CHAPTER FIVE
G.I. BLUES

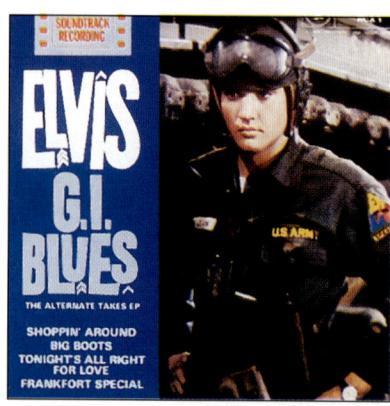

Even before he had joined the military, Elvis was bombarded with official offers. The navy offered the inducement of his serving exclusively with Memphis men, while the army offered less arduous duties than expected of normal recruits. The Pentagon was keen for Elvis to join what was known as the Special Services Unit, which consisted of entertainers who performed to the troops and undertook public relations exercises for the services.

Elvis refused all offers. 'I'm in the army. That's my job right now,' he declared. He was given the number 53310761 and was set to take whatever chances the army could offer him.

Once the media had been allowed to film, photograph and record in minute detail the process of his induction, Elvis disappeared into the military system. He was sent to Fort Chaffee, Arkansas, for the necessary paperwork to be completed. Assigned to the Second Medium Tank Battalion, Elvis was transferred to Texas for his basic training. At first, his colleagues were uncertain how to cope with the prospect of a national star in their midst. But within a few weeks it became clear that Elvis was unlikely to be taking advantage of special privileges and they grew both to like and respect him.

Elvis did, however, take advantage of one perquisite open to all drafted men. They were allowed to live off base provided their families were within easy reach. Most draftees on $78 a month could only afford this if their families genuinely lived nearby, but Elvis was receiving perhaps $300,000 a month and could afford to bring his parents out to him. There was an added factor in that his adored mother was ill and this may have contributed to his decision to keep the family together by renting a house close to base. On 10 June 1958, Elvis's first official leave of absence became due which allowed him to travel away from the immediate vicinity of his base camp. Colonel Parker ordered him to Nashville to cut some tracks.

King Creole opened in July 1958 and it was because of this film that Elvis was finally able to silence his critics and earn himself a respectable reputation as a movie actor rather than as a singer in a movie. The press gave good reviews, while Presley fans turned out in force as before. In fact, sales of Elvis records increased after he joined the army.

Nevertheless, Colonel Parker was well aware that his greatest-ever musical discovery was in trouble. It was quite on the cards that Elvis would be posted to some inaccessible part of the world where recording would be impossible. Even if based on the mainland United States, Elvis would be unable to give performances. The Colonel had to rely on all his publicity acumen for the next two years.

Elvis's induction had been something of a media frenzy with photographers and reporters covering every aspect of an unremarkable first day in the army. Perhaps predictably, they concentrated on Elvis having his infamous hair razored off to be replaced with a crew cut. The Colonel made certain that reporters emphasized how Elvis was about to serve his country like the good patriotic boy that he was and parents began to wonder if they had misjudged their teenagers' idol.

As for the musical output, without which any star would quickly fade, the Colonel had that sorted out as well. RCA Victor had plenty of tracks which Elvis had cut, but which had not been released. There were also the old Sun recordings which had received only limited distribution. By timing the release of these songs carefully, the Colonel considered that he could cover the two years Elvis would be away. Although there would be no shows or television

Elvis poses in army uniform. His tour of duty in the military proved to be a turning point for Elvis. His willingness to do his patriotic duty, and face the 'red menace' of communism in Germany, earned him the respect of an older generation which had previously regarded him as a dangerous influence on their teenagers.

G.I. Blues

ABOVE
Elvis (ringed) in the company of his army colleagues.

RIGHT
Elvis sports the sergeant's stripes which he worked so hard to earn during this two years in the army. Elvis was recognized as an exemplary soldier, keen to perform his duties as well as possible.

appearances, the Colonel's publicity skills ensured that Elvis stories were fed to the press to coincide with record releases. Only time would tell if Elvis fans would remain loyal to a star they could no longer see on stage or screen.

In July, the last thing the Colonel ever would have wished for, happened. Gladys, who had been unwell for some time, collapsed and was taken to hospital in Memphis. On 11 August her doctors sent for Elvis, who was granted immediate compassionate leave. Elvis flew straight to Memphis and raced to the hospital where Gladys had been diagnosed as suffering from hepatitis. The doctors believed the illness to have been caused by a liver complaint linked to heavy drinking and it is ironic that this may have been partly due to the success of her own beloved son. All she had ever wanted was for Elvis to be happy and successful. She cared for his every need and had devoted her life to him. But as the hoped-

for success grew ever greater, Elvis had spent more and more time away from home, causing Gladys to see him less and less. Loneliness and depression may well have been responsible for her descent into alcoholism.

Whatever brought on the illness, Gladys was clearly sinking fast. On the evening of 13 August, Elvis visited his mother in hospital when she asked him to make sure that all the flowers that had arrived were not wasted, but given to other patients. A few hours later Gladys Presley died of heart failure, a complication of hepatitis.

Elvis was inconsolable. He sat on the stairs at Graceland that morning and openly wept. None of his friends could help him and it was days before Elvis was able to return to normal life. In many ways, he was never the same again: he refused to watch the movies in which Gladys had appeared and found it difficult to talk about her.

Among the many services Gladys had performed for her son was cooking his favourite foods. Almost without exception these were the calorie-laden fried foods popular among the farmers and factory workers of the Deep South and Gladys would have been familiar with them from her own impoverished background in rural Mississippi. A few days after his mother's death, Elvis asked his home help to prepare for him a peanut butter sandwich and, on producing it, saw that Elvis was clearly disappointed. He took the woman down to the kitchen and showed her the way his mother would have made it. After buttering the bread and piling on the peanut butter, the snack was fried in a pan of bubbling fat until it was golden brown and crisp. While he was young and active, Elvis burned off the calories such rich foods provided but, later in life, he would suffer from increasingly serious weight problems. A diet designed for a hard life share-cropping in the hot Mississippi sun was simply out of the question for a man who spent much of his day relaxing or singing.

After 20 days' leave, Elvis was recalled to his unit. He was to go overseas, to Germany, to join the front line armoured troops protecting the Western democracies. Colonel Parker was delighted: he tipped off the press as to the time Elvis would be boarding ship in New York and arranged for a photo call on the dockside. RCA Victor managed to get Elvis alone for a few minutes during which he recorded interviews with reporters. These were later broadcast on radio and even released on disc. One feature of Elvis the soldier, which came as something of a shock to his fans, was his hair. Not only was it remarkably short, but it appeared to be brown. Few people had realized that his hair had been dyed black in his earlier days to match his black outfits and Elvis had kept it that way. The army was unwilling to condone such vanity, so Elvis's hair was allowed to revert to its natural colour and it is perhaps because of this that Elvis, while in the army, was nearly always photographed wearing a hat.

On 1 October 1958 the troopship P115 U.S.S. *General Randall* docked at Bremerhaven in Germany. It was the first time Elvis actually realized just how popular he was worldwide. A large crowd had gathered at the docks and when Elvis appeared on the gangway, the crowd surged forward with such force that the military

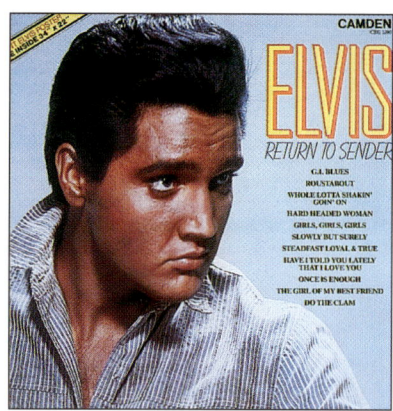

G.I. Blues

police had trouble holding them back. Elvis and the other troops were hurriedly bundled onto a train and removed from the scene. However, now that he was stationed abroad as part of an active unit, Elvis was finally left alone by the press to get on with his military service.

Meanwhile, Colonel Parker had no intention of letting Elvis fade from view. When *King Creole* had finished playing the cinemas and the sales of the soundtrack album had fallen off, the Colonel released a new album called *Elvis; For LP Fans Only*. It contained a collection of old recordings such as *Mystery Train*, *That's All Right* and *You're Right, I'm Left, She's Gone*. Hitting the stores in the spring of 1959, the album sold well, demonstrating that Elvis fans were as loyal as ever. Another indication of Elvis's enduring appeal was the amount of post received from fans. Some letters went to RCA Victor, while others were sent to his base in Germany and during his first few weeks there, some 40,000 letters a month were received. Although this staggering total began to decline slightly as the months passed, the monthly total never dipped below 20,000.

Elvis had brought his Memphis Mafia, including Red West and Lamar Fike, out to Germany with him, together with father Vernon and grandmother Minnie Presley. The entourage took a fine house in Bad Neuheim, near the base. Other servicemen, particularly officers, had their families in local accommodation, among them Sergeant Bill Stanley, with his wife Dee and three sons, and Captain Joseph Beaulieu and his adopted daughter Priscilla; both families were to feature prominently in the Presley future. One face from the past appearing in Germany was Captain Keisker. As receptionist Marion Keisker, she had been part of Sun studios when Elvis recorded that first disc for his mother's birthday.

In the meantime, Elvis spent his time much like any other serviceman. His duties included maintaining and driving a jeep (his love of automobiles made this a pleasure) and a surprise inspection of the 4th Armored Division revealed that Presley's was one of the few vehicles to achieve full marks for care and maintenance. He made frequent trips in the surrounding countryside, driving officers or delivering packages and messages and was made a corporal soon afterwards. He was later to reach the rank of sergeant.

While Colonel Parker was releasing a second album of old tracks, this time titled *A Date with Elvis*, Elvis was sent on field manoeuvres with his tank battalion near the border with the Communist East. As well as driving his jeep, Elvis had managed to become a crack shot and even to win an award for marksmanship. The manoeuvres were as close to battle conditions as training could get, including living out in the open for days on end, going without sleep and being continually subjected to stress. It is thought that during this time Elvis may have taken stimulants to help him cope with lack of sleep. Prescribed drugs were not unusual in the armed forces, and most young men were able to use them without long-term ill effects. If Elvis did use such drugs, he may well have developed a habit which would cost him so much in later life.

On a more promising note was Elvis's growing friendship with Priscilla Beaulieu. The

Elvis

LEFT
Elvis takes a meal in the mess alongside other servicemen.

BELOW
Elvis is interviewed by a female officer in his later days in the army. Unlike many other enlisted men, Elvis was in little need of the usual help with future civilian employment and qualifications which his comrades in arms would have received.

G.I. Blues

RIGHT
Vernon Presley inspects one of several awards his son won in the army for activities as varied as sharpshooting and jeep maintenance. Elvis enjoyed his time in the army and approached the task with the no-nonsense attitude: 'I'm in the army. That's my job right now.'

girl was intelligent, undeniably pretty, and very young. Indeed her youth soon led to difficulties for she was only 14. Her step-father was understandably protective and soon put his foot down regarding their liaison. If his daughter was to see the young soldier, it would be on his terms and, among other conditions, it was stipulated that Elvis should call himself and not send one of the Memphis Mafia to pick Priscilla up for dates.

But there could be no doubting the genuineness of Elvis's attraction for the girl. He told his relatives that his mother would have adored Priscilla – the first time this had been claimed of any date – and members of the entourage began to realize that they needed to take the young lady seriously and become accustomed to having her around. Elvis's father, too, embarked on a romantic attachment with Dee Stanley, Sergeant Stanley having previously obtained a divorce from his wife.

Meanwhile, the date of Elvis's discharge in March 1960 was getting closer. The latest album of old tracks had the remarkably unsubtle title of *50,000,000 Elvis Fans Can't Be Wrong*. It was the last gasp for this previously recorded material which by this point was beginning to sound rather old-fashioned as the rock and roll revolution progressed.

However, sales were strong, and it was clear that Elvis was still a major draw. Colonel Parker decided that when Elvis got home he would need to record an album and some singles as quickly as possible, and Hollywood was clamouring for another movie. The Colonel booked studio time for Elvis just three weeks after his discharge, and the movie was put into production in Elvis's absence.

It was decided that the movie should be based on Elvis's experiences in the army. Effectively, it followed the successful format of *Loving You*, putting Elvis into a role very close

LEFT
Elvis enjoys a break at a show. During his army days, Elvis was banned from undertaking any work other than for the military. This effectively blocked his recording and film career and even made it difficult for photographers to take formal publicity shots. Candid shots taken on the few occasions Elvis appeared in public were, however, acceptable and there was an insatiable demand for them.

BELOW
Elvis inspects a magazine article about himself with Swedish rock 'n' roll singer Little Gerhard. Although officially out of the public eye during his army years, Elvis remained the subject of press attention.

to his real life, but with a fictional story line to allow for dramatic content. Hal Wallis was brought in as producer while Juliet Prowse, Robert Ivers and Leticia Roman were to support Elvis in front of the camera. Scenes in which Elvis did not feature were shot, together with location shots of American troops and cast members in Germany; several scenes in which Elvis was supposed to appear on location were shot with a double, seen from behind. The Colonel wanted the movie in the cinemas as quickly as possible, so all that needed to be done was to shoot the Elvis scenes and produce the final cut. To keep the fans happy, and to prepare the way for the new movie, *Jailhouse Rock* was re-released.

On 1 March, the army threw a special farewell party for Elvis at the base in Freiburg. The next day he boarded an aircraft along with several other men due for discharge. At the airport Priscilla appeared to wave goodbye, this

being the first time the public or press had seen her, or realized that Elvis may have formed any romantic attachments in Germany. The mystery girl was at once dubbed 'The Girl He Left Behind' and a clamour began for as much information about her and the relationship as possible.

At his first interview in America, a reporter asked if Elvis had found himself a girlfriend while abroad. Elvis at once answered that he had not, then immediately corrected himself. *'There was a girl I was seeing quite often over there. Her father was in the air force and she was at the airport when I left and there were some pictures made of her. But it was no big romance.'* Clearly Elvis was ill at ease during this exchange and with good reason. Never one to tell lies, Elvis nevertheless knew the pressures media attention could impose and clearly wished to shield Priscilla and her family. There was also the fact that the two were separated by an ocean and that the attraction might not endure.

More importantly, the Colonel cannot have failed to be concerned by Priscilla's age, now 15. Only a few months earlier the rising rock star, Jerry Lee Lewis, had seen his career thrown into reverse amid the scandal of his marriage to a 13-year-old cousin. Nobody wished to see Elvis go the same way and it seemed best all round to allow Priscilla to fade from public view, no matter what the truth of the situation may have been.

On 5 March, amid a vast media hype orchestrated by the Colonel, Elvis left the army in New Jersey. The Colonel's intention was to show that Elvis had done his duty like a regular all-American boy. If Elvis was to continue to be a major star he would have to shed his rebellious and dangerous reputation of two years before. The army was happy to go along with the various interviews and press calls, being eager to show that being drafted was not the nightmare some young men believed it to be. If Elvis gave the impression that two years in the military was straightforward and enjoyable and, more importantly, not fatal to a career, then all to the good. At an interview, Elvis was asked what was the most important thing to have happened to him in the army. 'The biggest thing is, I did make it. I made it just like everybody else. Y'know. I tried to play it straight.'

So effective was the publicity drive that the train carrying Elvis home to Memphis became a major attraction for teenagers and pressmen at every town it visited. Even more impressive, given Elvis's previous reputation, was that the Mississippi House of Representatives passed a motion declaring Elvis *'...an inspiration to millions of Americans and hence reaffirms an historic American ideal that success in our nation can still be attained through individual initiative, hard work and abiding faith in oneself and in the Creator.'*

When Elvis returned to Graceland, he took off his uniform and carefully put it into storage – he was a civilian and a music star once again. He celebrated with a large cake in the shape of a guitar inscribed 'Welcome Home Elvis'.

Elvis

ABOVE
Elvis on board the troopship U.S.S. *General Randall* which took him to Germany to begin his active service.

BELOW LEFT
Elvis carries his kit bag on his first day in the army. Press photographers were allowed to record the day, but then had to abandon Elvis as he disappeared into the army machine.

LEFT
Elvis hugs a friend at Fort Hood in Texas where he underwent training in his chosen specialist duties – the motorized division responsible for transporting senior officers and important deliveries.

CHAPTER SIX
A CAREER IN MOVIES

The Graceland to which Elvis returned in 1960 was very largely his own creation, and the only house he ever really considered to be home. Although the house was remodelled several times, it is now much as it was in the 1960s – and pretty spectacular it is, too.

The drawing-room has a graceful charm, with its dark blue curtains edged in gold. Stained glass panels, featuring stylized peacocks, section off a part of the room, and it is here that a grand piano is housed. On more than one occasion, when Elvis had some hard thinking to do, it was to this piano that he came. As grand as the drawing-room is charming, the dining-room is a study in contrasts. The pure white carpeted floor has a large black marble central panel on which stands the dining-table and chairs, the table having a mirror top to reflect the heavy crystal chandelier that hangs above it. Around the walls are alcoves and cabinets in which silver and glass objects are displayed.

Another piano stands in the music-room, a serious workroom decorated in red. It was on this piano that Elvis would toy with tunes, working out the styles and arrangements which would set off his voice to the best effect. Outside this room, a staircase climbs to the first floor. Here the walls are covered in large mirrors into one of which a portrait of Elvis is set. In his will, Elvis stipulated that members of his family could live at Graceland for as long as they wished; his aunt Delta-May still does, occupying a suite of rooms on the upper floor. Although most of the house and grounds are now open to the public, access to the upstairs is forbidden in obedience to Elvis's last wishes.

The public are, however, permitted to enter the basement. It was here that Elvis allowed his imagination to run riot with the famous Jungle Room. The story goes that Elvis was watching TV one afternoon when he spotted an advertisement for Hawaiian furniture. He at once called the store and asked them if they would stay open late that night so that he could stop by to select a few items. When Elvis arrived he did much more than that: he virtually bought out the entire stock.

Among the more bizarre items were footstools and thrones shaped like half-moons several feet high, covered in fur and decorated with wooden carvings of ancient gods. Elvis

OPPOSITE
Elvis as Jess Wade, the reformed outlaw, in the movie *Charro*. The film caused quite a stir at the time of its release in 1969 because of a violent scene in which Elvis is branded with a red hot iron by old bandit buddies who believe he has double-crossed them.

A Career in Movies

RIGHT

Elvis belts out a number in the movie *G.I. Blues*. In the movie Elvis plays an American soldier stationed in Germany and desperately saving money to open a nightspot.

RIGHT

Elvis discusses the finer points of the script of *G.I. Blues* with the producer Hal Wallis. His first film after two years in the army, the movie was vital to Elvis's career and great care was taken with the songs, dialogue and shooting.

also collected hunting trophies and such memorabilia, but the masterstroke was the decor of the room in which the furniture was set. To give it that special jungle look, Elvis had the floor and ceiling covered in thick, dark-green carpet. One entire wall is occupied by a stone sculpture through which water flows and from which plants sprout, recreating a mountain stream tumbling down into a densely forested chasm.

One of the extensions added to the house by Elvis was intended to be a games room, but before long Elvis was using it to house trophies, hanging the walls with his gold and platinum discs, together with his Grammy awards, favourite stage outfits and various souvenirs, including a letter from President Nixon; there was even a china hound dog.

Many people who knew Elvis consider that Graceland gives a revealing insight into his mind and personality, the exuberant Jungle Room showing as much a part of his character as the coolly elegant dining-room. When a man has both time and money to fully indulge his tastes, it is hardly surprising that the end result should hold a mirror up to Elvis's inner self.

Elvis relied ever more on his home as a place to which he could retreat as his career developed, involving as it did so much travelling and hard work, all of it orchestrated by Colonel Parker. First on the schedule was an extensive series of recording sessions at the RCA Studios in Nashville, which lasted from March into May. No less than 32 songs were recorded in these busy weeks, including some of the all-time Elvis classics. *Wooden Heart, Fever, It's Now or Never, G.I. Blues* and *Tonight is So Right for Love* were all discs cut at this time.

It was clear to all concerned that Elvis had lost none of his magic; indeed he had acquired more dynamism and maturity. In many ways, these sessions were extensions of the final recordings he made before Germany. He had the same band as before and many of the musical techniques and styles were as they had been two years previously. Because several of the songs were destined for the soundtrack of the movie *G.I. Blues*, there is a strong European flavour to some of them. *Wooden Heart* is taken from a German folk song while *Tonight is So*

In a scene from *G.I. Blues*, Elvis jokes with his army buddies as they hatch a plot to trick a local cabaret performer, played by Juliet Prowse. The plan goes horribly wrong, landing Elvis in all kinds of trouble before the plot is finally resolved.

A Career in Movies

Elvis sings the theme song to the movie *Love Me Tender* in a scene at the beginning of the movie. The song became so popular when released as a single, that the film was hurriedly re-edited to feature the song again at the close of the action.

Right for Love takes a tune from an Offenbach opera and *It's Now or Never* is an adaptation of the old Italian love song *O Sole Mio*. All three are beautifully adapted by Elvis, the first and last maintaining a gently romantic flavour, while the second was somewhat rocked up.

During this busy schedule, Elvis found the time to travel to Florida to record a television show entitled *Welcome Home Elvis*. The show was one of a series of programmes hosted by Frank Sinatra, and many people wondered how two such very different entertainers would get along together as, back in 1957, Sinatra had made some extremely unflattering comments concerning Elvis and his music.

In the event, the liaison was successful; Sinatra appeared in a classic evening suit, while Elvis wore an outfit of a more modern cut, with tucked down tie. Elvis was paid a staggering $125,000 for the show, in which he sang just two songs on his own. At the end of the show he appeared with Sinatra in a curious duet in which the two singers alternated with each other, singing lines from each others' songs. Sinatra sang Love *Me Tender* in his style, while Elvis belted out *Witchcraft*, using some standard Sinatra body movements for good measure. The show was judged a success and got Elvis back into the public eye in a big way.

Also packed into these busy weeks was the shooting of *G.I. Blues*. Based on the experiences of Elvis and many thousands of other draftees to Europe, the movie was pushed through at great speed, some scenes having already been shot while Elvis was in the army. Produced by Hal Wallis, who had masterminded the pre-army Paramount movies, the film was directed by Norman Taurog. This was the first time Elvis had worked with this director, but it would be far from the last.

The first Elvis movie after his discharge from the army was bound to be major news, and the filming attracted much attention. Foreign royalty came to see the work in production and the press clamoured for details of the movie and its shooting. One feature of the activities which came out later was that Elvis had more than a professional interest in his co-star, Juliet Prowse. Prowse, at the time, was dating Frank Sinatra who was understandably less than impressed to realize that his recent TV guest was trying to muscle in. It is said that Sinatra got some tough guys to pay a visit to Elvis to warn him off. Whatever the truth of the story, Elvis did not become permanently involved with Prowse.

In the midst of filming, Vernon Presley

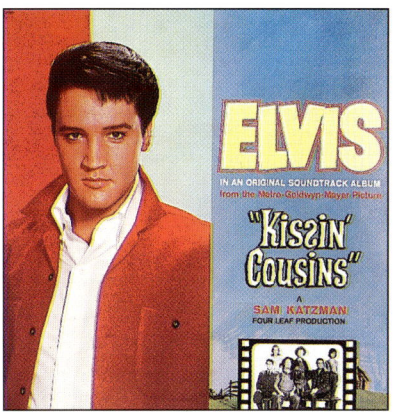

LEFT

Elvis on the set of the movie *Love Me Tender*. The movie was originally entitled *The Reno Brothers* with Richard Egan as the star. The casting of Elvis as Egan's younger brother and the timing of the release on disc of the songs Elvis sang in the movie led to the change of title, though Egan retained his star billing with Elvis's name prefixed 'Introducing' on official publicity.

A Career in Movies

As the Elvis movies were rolled out his character became almost stereotypical as a young and talented singer with something of a disreputable past who wins out in the end. Above: Elvis plays a pilot in trouble with the Federal Aviation Agency in *Paradise – Hawaiian Style*. Left: In *Change of Habit*, Elvis's 31st movie, he plays a doctor in the slums of Puerto Rico. Opposite: The movie *Girls, Girls, Girls*, made in 1962, features Elvis as an impoverished fisherman desperate to scrape together the funds to buy a top-class fishing boat.

A Career in Movies

informed his son that he wished to remarry. The bride-to-be was Dee Stanley, whom the Presleys had met in Germany. To some it seemed that Vernon was almost asking his son's permission to get married. Although Elvis's feelings can only be guessed at, it is clear that he was surprised that Vernon was able to recover from Gladys's death so quickly. Elvis would never entirely come to terms with the loss of his mother and was somewhat perturbed that Vernon had so quickly found someone to take his wife's place.

Elvis did not attend the wedding, which took place in Alabama on 3 July, the Colonel explaining that Elvis was busy in Hollywood. In any case, the wedding was a private affair

By 1967 the Elvis movies, though fun and entertaining, had got the King into something of a rut. Attempts to update the image with 1960s-style attitudes only served to highlight the need for Elvis to return to giving live performances.

A Career in Movies

for the happy couple and if Elvis had turned up it would have degenerated into a media scrum. But many suspected that Elvis was upset by the whole business and simply preferred not to attend.

The new movie was released in October, to scenes of wild enthusiasm – and to complimentary reviews. The *Hollywood Reporter* said that ' ...it was a subdued and changed Elvis Presley who has returned from the military service in Germany to star in Hal Wallis's *G.I. Blues*', and this was intended as a compliment from those who had disapproved of his earlier wild image. Elvis's movie persona is very different from the brooding, tortured figure of *King Creole*; he plays with children, makes

good, and is an all-round nice guy.

The film was, in truth, well made and professional. The story of the draftee struck a chord with many who had undergone similar experiences: the songs were catchy and Elvis was in fine fettle as both actor and singer. The movie was a hit, which encouraged Paramount to put their next Elvis movie into the cinemas as quickly as possible.

Flaming Star was released in December, but was based on a very different theme and one not many Elvis fans were likely to appreciate. For a start, there were only two songs, and one of these was played over the credits. The storyline, also, was rather difficult. Made at the height of the Civil Rights movement, the film explored the theme of racial intolerance. Elvis plays a half-breed Native American living with his white father's family in the old West. When a band of Indians kills a family of settlers, the local community turns against Elvis, who eventually returns to his native roots.

Elvis acts extremely well in *Flaming Star*. Indeed this is arguably his finest piece ever. Director Don Siegel handles the plot and its tense undertones in a sensitive way, as do the supporting cast of Steve Forrest, Barbara Eden and Dolores Del Rio. In itself the movie is a good one, but it was not what Elvis fans wanted to see as there was no dancing and precious little singing from their idol. Although the film made a profit, it failed to do particularly well.

Colonel Parker learned his lesson from *Flaming Star*. Elvis might be a good actor, but he had made his name as a truly outstanding singer and dancer. That was what Elvis did best and what his fans required. The next movie, *Wild in the Country*, was also a drama, but four songs were worked into the film to keep the fans happy. Made by 20th Century Fox, it is a gentle romance which did not particularly stretch Elvis's acting ability, but the part was good enough to earn decent reviews.

Elvis on stage in the movies. Although the movies almost invariably featured at least one scene with Elvis on stage, driving an audience wild, the truth was very different. Scenes were shot over and over, and the audiences were as much actors as Elvis himself. Elvis began to worry that he was losing his ability to work a live audience.

75

A Career in Movies

Elvis and co-star Jo Symington in the culminating scene of the movie *Easy Come, Easy Go* in which Elvis plays a U.S. Navy diver who uses his spare time to search for a chest of gold coins which was lost in a shipwreck some years earlier and which had belonged to Symington's grandfather.

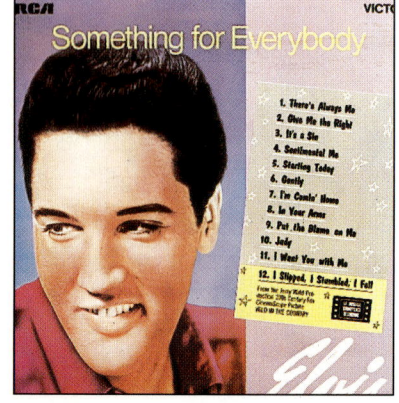

After the hectic filming schedule came to an end, Elvis insisted on a project he had been considering for some time: he wished to record an album of religious music. Released as *His Hand in Mine*, the album goes right back to Elvis's childhood when he attended church with his mother and hung around outside churches where black music was performed. The songs range from the sentimental *Jesus Knows Just What I Need* to the revivalist *Working on the Building* and the spiritual *Joshua Fit the Battle*. The complete album displays the range of styles and emotions Elvis was capable of injecting into his work; the subject matter, though in the mainstream of Memphis country music-making was, however, very different from the rock music expected by worldwide audiences. Sales, though hardly disappointing, were not exactly huge.

The next album returned to the rock style required by the public. *Something for Everybody* includes the tracks from the movie *Wild in the Country*, together with other tracks recorded in Nashville in March 1961. Although the great Floyd Cramer backed Elvis on the piano, the album is not generally considered to be among Elvis's finest.

Meanwhile, back in the movies, Elvis was hitting the spot with a movie so successful that it was to set the pattern for years to come. The movie was *Blue Hawaii* and it contained almost everything that an Elvis fan could wish for: Elvis sang no less than 14 songs – all set in a beautiful and exotic location. Moreover, Elvis plays a character not too far distant from himself as a previously poor young musician who eventually makes good. The producer was Hal Wallis, who put together a classic team. Norman Taurog was brought back as director and the screenplay was by Hal Kante. Joseph Lilley was credited with the music score, though in truth Elvis did much of the arranging.

The co-stars included Angela Lansbury and Joan Blackman, both top-rank actresses.

The final result was a triumph both in terms of artistic excellence and box office returns. Elvis fans flocked to see their hero, very much on musical form, while the exotic locations guaranteed a visual feast. The music was something of a tricky proposition as the task of producing rock and roll with Hawaiian undertones was no easy matter. In the event, the most successful numbers in the film are those which are either pure Hawaiian, including the title track *Blue Hawaii,* or straight rock and roll such as *Slicing Sand. Rock-a-Hula Baby*, the only genuine attempt at fusing rock with Hawaiian is good enough, but fails to reach the heights of which Elvis was capable.

So staggeringly successful was the movie that Hollywood soon came to the conclusion that it had hit upon a winning formula and for eight years saw no reason to vary it. Elvis would star as a poor but transparently honest boy who worked hard and got a lucky break to become a success by the end of the movie; the Elvis Movie became almost a genre in itself, alongside horror, western and detective films. Most movies gave a nod in the direction of Elvis's bad-boy image of the 1950s by having him involved in a fight or two, though only when the other guy was clearly in the wrong. The soundtrack always featured a number of songs by Elvis, which were released as an album alongside the movie, and some hit the shops as singles. Colonel Parker kept a close

Cashing in on the earlier success of the movie *Blue Hawaii*, the inferior 1966 film *Paradise – Hawaiian Style*, teamed Elvis with Suzanna Leigh as the love interest.

A Career in Movies

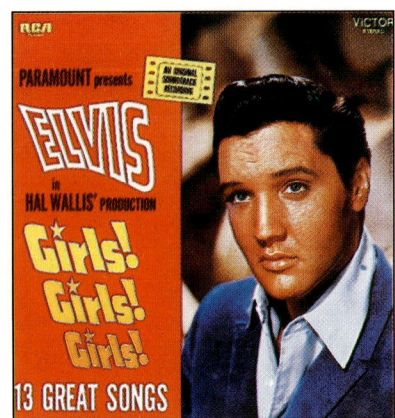

eye on the movies and their scripts: he refused to let Elvis play characters who did illegal or evil things, or indulged in such vices as drinking or cursing.

By the time *Girls, Girls, Girls* hit the big screen in 1962 the pattern was well established. Norman Taurog directed Elvis alongside Stella Stevens and Laurel Goodwin. Although undeniably attractive and good actresses, the girls were not likely to take the limelight away from Elvis. The dance routines were spectacular, including exotic South Sea settings, but they lacked the innovation and raw power of *Jailhouse Rock*. The poster for the movie not only made much of Elvis, the girls and the music, but was quite explicit about the album which had been released and which contained the soundtrack songs. The film included the great classic, *Return to Sender*, one of the best songs to come out of the Elvis movies of the 1960s.

It is usual to sneer at these films and write them off as mindless pap. It is true that compared to the dramatic intensity of *King Creole* or *Flaming Star* they make little demand on Elvis's acting abilities and some suffer from the effects of weak scripts and mediocre songs. However, that is to miss the point. The films were not intended to be great dramas, nor even classic musicals. They were meant to be a showcase, a vehicle for Elvis and his talents in a format that would reach the largest number of people without putting undue stress on the star. The only real problem is that there were so many films and they all looked so very much the same and by 1968, it was only Elvis fans who wished to see them. Everyone knew in advance what the plot would be, the style of music and dance, and could even make a good guess at the characterization.

As far as fans were concerned, the films were successful. They were bouncy, fun and showed off their hero to the best effect. They made a great deal of money for the studios, and enabled Elvis to establish his fortune. He was paid a flat fee of $1 million for each movie, plus a share of the profits and, of course, the revenue from the record sales. Today, the majority of these films seem just as frothy and enjoyable as when they were first made and it is difficult to think of higher praise for light musicals made specifically to highlight a single talent.

But if the movies were predictable, Elvis's personal life was not. It took a great deal of imagination and skill on Colonel Parker's part to keep Elvis in the headlines for the right reasons rather than the wrong ones, and without recourse to downright lies. As in Germany, it was Priscilla who was at the centre of interest.

In October 1962, Priscilla came to live at Graceland. Although 'The Girl He Left Behind' had dropped right out of newspaper stories since Elvis's denial of a relationship, she still continued to be very much on his mind. Despite several short romances with various actresses, Elvis had failed to find anyone to replace Priscilla in his affections. He wrote her frequent letters and made many phone calls and by December 1960 had invited Priscilla to fly to America and spend Christmas at Graceland. Captain Beaulieu was hardly enthralled by the idea, his step-daughter being still only 15, and Beaulieu had read newspaper reports of Elvis's

Elvis strums his guitar in the 1957 classic movie *Jailhouse Rock*. The character, Vince Everett, is an impoverished youngster who is blamed for a death in a bar brawl and sent to prison. There he learns to sing and dance, ensuring his fame and fortune on finishing his sentence.

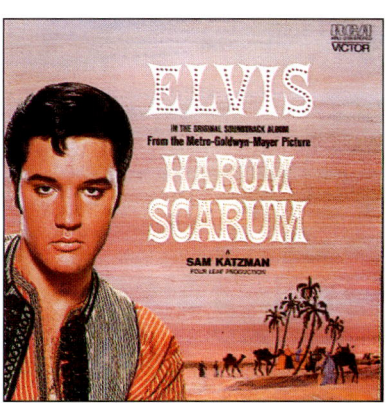

A Career in Movies

many relationships as much as anyone else. It was one thing to let a teenage girl go on dates with a clean-cut soldier, quite another to allow her to stay in the home of a notorious rock star.

It apparently took a lot of persistence on Elvis's part to make the Captain change his mind. It helped that Beaulieu knew Vernon's new wife and Elvis's grandmother, both of whom were living at Graceland. It was finally agreed that Priscilla could spend Christmas at Graceland, but only on the understanding that she would be strictly chaperoned by the two older women. And the Captain insisted on knowing what was going on the whole time. The visit lasted only a few days, but it seems to have been enough for both Elvis and Priscilla, and letters and phone calls became even more frequent over the following months.

In 1961 Captain Beaulieu was promoted to major and posted to California. By the following summer, Presley was becoming impatient to have Priscilla with him in Memphis. The Major, however, was as opposed to his daughter moving in with Elvis as he had been about her Christmas visit. She was now 17, but was still at high school. Quite naturally, the Major did not want her to become too heavily involved in what might turn out to be a teenage crush. By the time Elvis had found a good, respectable Catholic high school in Memphis, altered his domestic arrangements to suit the Major's requirements, and had repeatedly emphasized his own moral rectitude and the views of his grandmother and stepmother, the Major gave in.

Colonel Parker was still as worried about Priscilla's extreme youth as he had been when

Possibly the most famous scene in any Elvis Presley movie is the great set-piece dance routine from *Jailhouse Rock*. With hindsight, the scene has come to be dubbed 'the first music video', but at the time it was simply a magnificent setting for Elvis to show his talents off to his fans. The choreography was largely Elvis's own work.

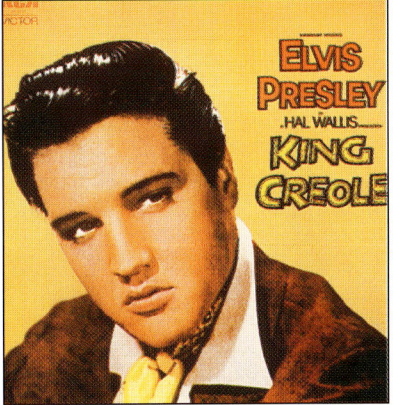

A Career in Movies

RIGHT
Elvis on stage for the set-piece *Trouble* in his TV Special of 1968. The scene was modelled on the famous *Jailhouse Rock* sequence and was intended to remind the viewing public of his earlier successes.

OPPOSITE
A dramatic publicity shot for *King Creole,* emphasizing the violence and moodiness of Elvis's character, Danny Fisher.

BELOW
Elvis with Walter Matthau, who played a sinister underworld boss in *King Creole*.

she was just 14. No announcement was made of the fact that Priscilla was joining the Graceland household: if anyone asked, they were told that Elvis was allowing the daughter of an old army pal to stay at his home while she finished her schooling in America. It was not exactly a lie, but neither was it entirely the truth. It was believed, however, and the romance was left to flourish in secret.

Elvis continued to produce musicals to a highly lucrative degree. Some years as many as three movies appeared, together with soundtrack albums and singles. In May 1966, Elvis decided to produce another religious album – the result, *How Great Thou Art* – winning him his first Grammy award, which meant a great deal to the singer and was a treasured possession. This album can be seen, with hindsight, to have been vital to Elvis's career. Rather than simply taking the money and performing songs provided for him, Elvis was singing what he himself wanted to sing, in arrangements suitable for him. The album won much critical acclaim, and was widely seen as a change of direction: many people felt it was about time.

While Elvis was stacking up a fortune producing films with rock and roll tracks, popular music was passing him by. In 1957 Elvis had been at the dangerous cutting edge of the developing teen music phenomenon. But by 1966 the music business was dominated by the Beatles, the Rolling Stones and other groups writing and performing their own material. As a performer of other peoples' music, Elvis was distinctly old-fashioned. His numbers were also beginning to sound rather dated as he continued to churn out songs which would keep his fans happy; but the fans were getting older and were no longer representative of the teenage market of the day.

It seemed as though the great star would simply fade away, or be relegated to hosting television shows. Elvis himself could hardly have been happy at the prospect of gradually falling record sales and increasingly less media attention; but Colonel Parker was unwilling to take any risks. The movies were still making healthy profits and to make drastic changes could well put all they had worked for in jeopardy. The year 1966 saw three films: the undistinguished *Paradise – Hawaiian Style*, together with *Spinout* and *Frankie and Johnny*. None of the singles released that year hit the magic $1 million sales figure.

Years later, a woman recalled meeting Elvis

A Career in Movies

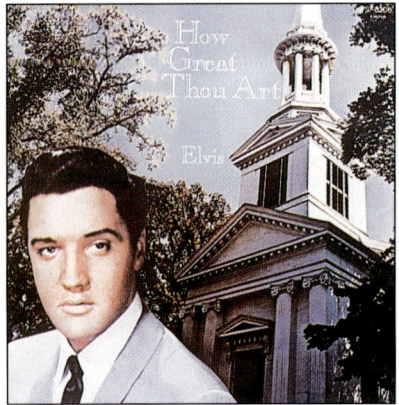

RIGHT
The wedding of Elvis to Priscilla was a relatively modest affair in Las Vegas to which only the couple's closest family and friends were invited. This did not prevent Elvis lavishing money on an elaborate cake and floral decoration.

while he was filming a western in Arizona, and offered her thoughts on the event. *'I was about nine years old when my mother dragged me from Flagstaff, Arizona, down to Sedona to camp out all day outside a bank where they were filming a scene from* Stay Away Joe. *I was too young to appreciate why I was being made to play in 90-degree heat in a ditch with the son of a friend of Mom's, and why my mother, her friend and her friend's daughter were doing nothing but standing around staring at a building. Eventually this man came out of the building and began signing little pieces of paper that were thrust at him. My mother didn't get an autograph, but Caroline, the friend's daughter, did. She also got a picture of her and him together.*

'Months later I got taken to the movie. "Do you remember seeing that man up there?", my mother asked me. I sort of made the connection, and sort of not. "He could sing anything, you know?", I recall Mom telling me. And she was right. Any style, any song. It's just too bad he got stuck in a fish bowl. And it's too bad Colonel Parker wouldn't let him off of the leash to do really good movies. And when you lock the world out, you're locked in.'

Developments were occurring in Elvis's personal life: Priscilla had left the Immaculate Conception High School and had attended the Patricia Stevens Finishing School. The attraction between the two was as strong as ever and there seemed no reason to keep it quiet any longer. On Christmas Eve 1966, Elvis proposed marriage and was accepted. The announcement was made after the holiday and was a surprise to everyone outside the couple's immediate circle of friends.

The wedding took place on 1 May 1967 at the Aladdin Hotel in Las Vegas. It was a surprisingly modest affair, with only a handful of family guests. Priscilla's younger sister, Michelle, was bridesmaid, while Elvis had two best men, Joe Esposito and Marty Lacker. Elvis was resplendent in a dark brocade tuxedo and sported a white carnation. Priscilla had her hair done in the fashionable bouffant style, dyed black to match Elvis's, and she wore a distinctive loose gown with beaded lace over the arms and shoulders.

The ceremony was held in private, as was the champagne reception which followed. The only concession to the vast media attention was a showy many-tiered cake, festooned with red roses and sugar hearts, which was a feature of the press call. A much larger party was held a few days later at Graceland for friends and business colleagues who had not been present in Las Vegas.

There could be no disguising Elvis's happiness at this point in his life. Many people have credited marriage to Priscilla with giving Elvis the impetus he needed to revitalize his languishing career. In September 1967 he returned to the RCA studios in Nashville for a major recording session spread over three days. Elvis was not recording for either a film or an album; he seems to have decided on the session

By the time Priscilla married Elvis, her appearance was very different from that of the fresh-faced teenager Elvis had met in Germany. Her dyed hair was piled into a fashionable bouffant and her eyes heavily made up.

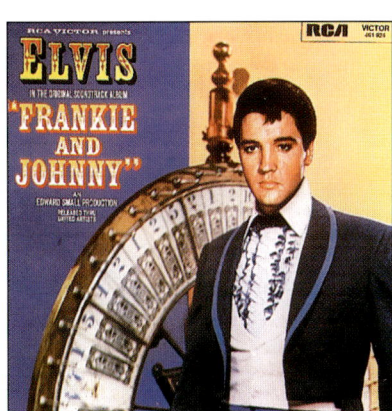

A Career in Movies

OPPOSITE
Elvis surrounded by fans in the 'pit segment' during his TV comeback special.

BELOW
Exactly nine months after their wedding, a baby daughter was born to Elvis and Priscilla. Many of his friends believed his happy marriage followed by Lisa Marie's birth was just the impetus Elvis needed to make his comeback to live performances which he had been contemplating for so long.

simply to try out new ideas and arrangements.

Floyd Cramer was on the piano with Jerry Reed on guitar and Charlie McCoy on other instruments. The songs were later released and it is possible to get a feel of what Elvis was trying to achieve. In some songs he experiments with the latest rock styles being thumped out by younger bands, but he cannot quite match their enthusiasm. In other songs he tries the Mersey Beat style made famous by the Beatles and Gerry and the Pacemakers. But he is at his best when he returns to his own roots in blues and country music. *Big Boss Man* exemplifies the best on this occasion and proves that Elvis was as capable as ever of producing exciting rock and roll.

In February 1968 Priscilla gave birth to Lisa Marie in Memphis. There could be no doubt that the event took Elvis's private life to a new high and he proved himself a devoted father, making as much time as possible for the child in his busy schedule. The increased happiness and enthusiasm for life spurred him on to new projects.

The first movie made after Lisa Marie's birth was *Live a Little, Love a Little*. There were only four songs in the film, but a great deal of care was put into the arranging and recording of them. The result is four songs which are superior to any of the songs in the preceding few movies.

Whether it was events in his family life, or a confidence born out of successful recording sessions, Elvis clearly decided to make a major change in his career which led him to his first disagreement for many years with Colonel Parker. At stake was Elvis's entire future as a performer of popular music. At the time, it was difficult to see who was right, or who would win the argument: Elvis was heading for a major gamble.

CHAPTER SEVEN
THE COMEBACK

When Elvis decided to stage a comeback and a return to live performances after his years in Hollywood, the question was how to do it. The vehicle chosen for the comeback was an hour-long television special due to go out in December 1968 on NBC. It was the format and style of this crucial show which led to disagreements between Elvis and Colonel Parker.

The trouble began when NBC appointed Steve Binder as director and producer of the show. Binder was much the same age as Elvis and had been a big fan in the 1950s when Elvis was daring and exciting. His wish was to recapture that rebellious feeling in a shift away from the play-safe attitudes of the movies. Colonel Parker disagreed: he was against Elvis taking any risks and saw the show as a way of getting Elvis on film, singing the songs that had made him famous, performing some of his beloved hymns, and perhaps doing a comic routine with another celebrity or two – also, of course, making a lot of money along the way.

Despite negotiations and efforts to reach a compromise by NBC, neither Steve Binder nor the Colonel would back down. It was up to

The Comeback

Having decided on a return to live performance, Elvis rose to the challenge with enthusiasm. Equipping a specially converted Greyhound bus to his needs, Elvis went on the road. At first his stage shows were very similar to the way they had been before he went into movies and his earlier preference for black clothes appears to have survived.

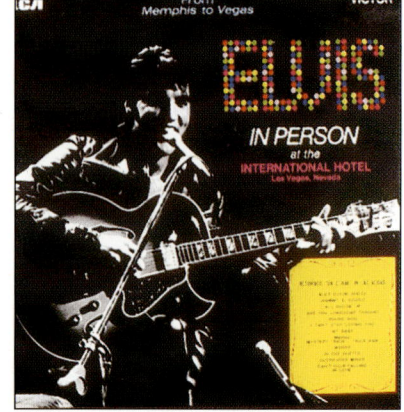

Elvis. Not since the stairwell recordings in his earliest RCA days had Elvis opposed the Colonel, but he instinctively felt that, from an artistic point of view, Binder was right and, since that was the whole reason for the comeback, Elvis backed Binder.

Rehearsals began, with the final show due to be recorded over a number of sessions beginning on 27 June. The idea was to have a number of big-set numbers to begin and end the show, with a more intimate section in between. It was this central section that Elvis viewed with trepidation and which took the most time to perfect.

Generally known during production as 'the pit segment', this had Elvis performing on a small square stage surrounded by banks of seating. Elvis was to stand alone with his guitar on stage, while the band played off stage. It was putting the entire burden of performance on Elvis as well as testing his ability to hold the attention of the audience, most of whom had never seen him perform live. After a few songs, Elvis was due to be joined on stage by the old Sun studio band of Scotty Moore and D. J. Fontana, another musician taking the place of Bill Black who had died in 1965. If anything was going to be a recreation of the 1950s, this was it.

It was the feeling of performing to a live audience that Elvis was keen to recapture. 'As the years went by I missed audience contact,' he said. 'I was really getting bugged. I couldn't do what I could do, y'know. They [film directors] would say "action" and I would go "uh-uh".'

Ironically, it was the prospect of a live

performance which had Elvis most deeply worried. Even with a studio audience as small and tame as this one, it had been eight years since he had got up in front of an audience and Elvis, more than any other performer, knew that stagecraft consisted of far more than merely singing well. To get a good audience reaction demanded an instinctive feel for people, an ability to read their emotions and be able to play upon them. In the 1950s, Elvis had had this ability so intuitively within his grasp that he rarely had to think about it; but time had elapsed and Elvis was having doubts. Elvis subjected himself to a tough training régime, endlessly practising the music and every movement which had first made him famous. He also went on a serious diet, shedding the pounds in the hope of regaining his slim physique of the 1950s.

As rehearsals ended and the day of the performance arrived, everyone began to show

signs of nerves. Although the Colonel had been excluded from the artistic side of the show, he was still around to keep an eye on his boy. Ever the showman, he turned his attention to rearranging the audience so that pretty girls would be in line with the camera and would be guaranteed to appear more frequently on screen. Elvis, meanwhile, was pacing back and forth like a caged lion. By the time the lights went up he was visibly shaking as he strode out onto the stage.

In the event, the show was a triumph, with Elvis on top form. Scotty Moore, not having performed with Elvis for some time, was most impressed. Moore said later, 'In the '68 Special he was just as much like he was in the first years, '54 or '55, as you could ask him to be.' And he was right. There could be no doubt that this was the old Elvis, and entirely different from the characters he played in the movies.

After many months of editing, cutting and re-recording of some songs, the finished Special was ready for broadcast on 3 December 1968. Steve Binder had done his job well and it was clear that he had correctly gauged the signs of the times where Elvis was concerned.

The show opened in bold fashion. In silence, a neon light traced the word ELVIS across the screen. At once the band cut in with the distinctive opening of *Trouble* and when the screen faded to black it was replaced with a close-up of Elvis's face as he spat out the opening lines – 'If you're looking for trouble, you came to the right place. If you're looking for trouble, it's right here in my face.' Dramatic stuff, indeed!

As Elvis came to the end of that first number, the camera pulled back to reveal a set entirely composed of the letters ELVIS in 20-foot (6-metre) high red neon. No sooner had the viewer grasped what it was then on came dozens of dancers, all of them dressed like

As Elvis gained more experience of the touring scene of the late 1960s, he began to change his image. The earlier preference for casual outdoor clothes with turned-up collars became exaggerated and formalized into the startling jumpsuits with the tall, stand-up collars which were to become Elvis's trademark in his later years.

The Comeback

Elvis. The song *Guitar Man* was illustrated by the fact that every dancer had a guitar strung around their necks.

Most people agree, however, that it is 'the pit segment' where the show really comes to life. Dressed in an all-black leather jumpsuit, Elvis threw himself completely into the music, gyrating and pulsating with all his old gusto. Then his band came on stage, and Elvis slipped easily into a more relaxed style as he joked and chatted to his old friends. Audience involvement was one of his well established stage techniques, and he made use of it again in this part of the show. In one of his more famous unscripted asides, he curled his lip into the familiar sneer, then joked, 'I've got news for you, I did 29 movies like that.'

The show ended with Elvis alone on stage, singing a number specially written for the show. *If I Can Dream* is a simple heartfelt plea that the world might become a better place. To some ears it may have sounded trite and naïve, but Priscilla later confirmed that it truly summed up Elvis's hopes for the future. Released as a single, the song turned out to be his biggest hit since 1965, eventually selling over a million copies. The album of the TV show also sold well, going gold within a few months.

The success of the TV special and the subsequent record sales was of great encouragement to Elvis. His planned comeback was bearing fruit and was clearly the way forward, although the Colonel continued to appear somewhat unconvinced. On 13 January 1969, Elvis arrived at the American Studios in Memphis for a marathon 10-day recording session and the following month he returned for

a further six more days of recording.

The songs to come out of these two sessions were to mark a real turning point in the singer's career. The most significant was *Suspicious Minds* which went all the way to the number 1 slot on the Billboard charts and another track, *In The Ghetto*, went to number 3. Suddenly Elvis was a major rock star once more, and had the record sales to prove it. Among the more experimental songs he recorded was a version of the Beatles song, *Hey Jude*, reworked so completely as to be almost unrecognizable to anyone familiar with the original. The majority of the songs were, however, mainstream rock or country tracks of the type Elvis had mastered and made his own.

Elvis was keen to build on his growing success away from frothy musical movies. Having conquered television and the recording studio, serious acting was next on the agenda. The film *Charro* was a Western without music in which Elvis was called upon to really act. The decision that Elvis should be bearded in

LEFT
Elvis with Sammy Davis Jnr. with security guard and old school friend Red West standing right behind them. Throughout his career, Elvis preferred the company of old friends to that of fellow celebrities. Only people Elvis genuinely liked were allowed to enter his small circle of friends and companions.

OPPOSITE
Elvis in one of his later and more colourful jumpsuits. The scarf around his neck was a regular feature of his stage act. After wiping his face with it, it would be tossed into the audience for some adoring fan to take home. During the average show he would get through several scarves in this way.

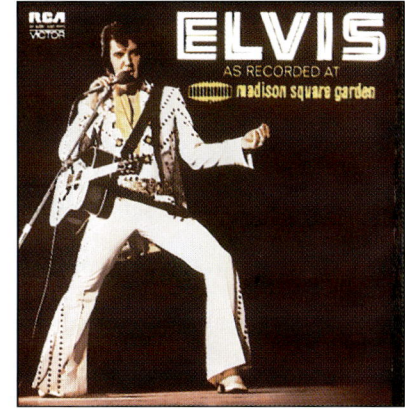

The Comeback

OPPOSITE

The famous 'Gypsy' jumpsuit worn by Elvis in the early 1970s. Some of the outfits worn on stage were given names and became Elvis's favourites, becoming equally popular with the fans.

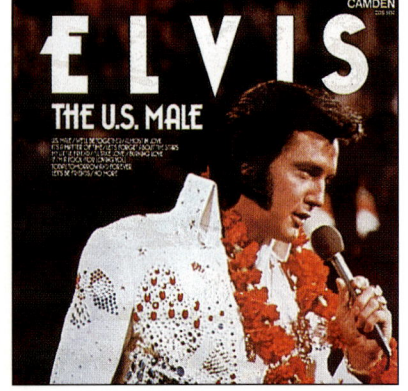

this movie was, with hindsight, something of a mistake. The intention may have been to make it crystal clear that this was a totally new departure, but all it did was distract attention from the performance. The beard was quickly removed, never to return, and serious acting was abandoned for good. After all, a new and far more exciting prospect was on the horizon – touring.

Colonel Parker had finally been won over by the continuing success of this new turn in Elvis's career and began to search for venues large enough to cope with the expected crowds. Then the Colonel received an offer he could not refuse. The new International Hotel in Las Vegas, though uncompleted, was looking for a major act with which to open and Elvis was offered $1 million for a two-week appearance.

But if the Las Vegas job struck the Colonel as too good to turn down, Elvis was not so sure. The only previous time he had appeared in Las Vegas had proved disastrous and he had no wish to repeat the experience. Only after repeated assurances that the Las Vegas audiences had changed, that he was now an established star, and that he could pick his own band, did Elvis finally agree.

But before Las Vegas, Elvis had one last film contract to fulfil. The final movie, *Change of Habit,* co-starred Mary Tyler Moore, and it was clear that Elvis was not really throwing himself wholeheartedly into the part. The songs (there were only four) were not top quality, although the fast rock number *Let Us Pray* was the best of the bunch from the recent movie compositions.

Filming finished in July, and Elvis travelled directly to Las Vegas where he put together the band which would appear with him on stage. Among the musicians were the veteran rock guitarist James Burton and the gospel singers Sweet Inspirations. The band undertook an intensive rehearsal period together with Elvis, who was determined that the new show would be as perfect as he could make it.

On 31 July Elvis was back on stage. As if to emphasize that it was his personal comeback, the show opened on a subdued setting on which a single spotlight played. Into the circle of light walked Elvis, guitar in hand, at which point the band sprang into life. His performance – all the critics agreed – was nothing short of stupendous. All thoughts that his live presence may have deteriorated were quelled. Although, in many ways, the Elvis of the Las Vegas shows was the old electrifying stage performer of the 1950s, this was a new Elvis – the Elvis that many people would continue to remember after his death.

Gone were the casual outdoor clothes with turned-up collar that Elvis had previously sported, as were the flashy pink, white and black country outfits. Instead, Elvis wore a jet-black suit with flared sleeves and a high collar. Though it would be a couple of years before this outfit developed into the colourful and glittering jumpsuits of later legend, the look was clearly evolving. Also beginning to appear were gestures which were to become Elvis trademarks. Elvis had always knelt at the front of the stage to talk to or even make contact with the first few rows of fans, but now these simple actions became exaggerated. One move to become a classic was to ask for a handkerchief, use it to wipe his face, and hand it back.

So successful were these Las Vegas shows that the International asked him to stay on for a further two weeks, then booked Elvis for a return trip in January. The January season of 29 shows was sold out almost before the tickets went on sale and a further 29 shows were scheduled. Elvis's appearances attracted so many people to Las Vegas that it was calculated that takings from tourists gambling, dining and drinking rose by an amazing 10 per cent when Elvis was performing.

Flushed with the success of the Las Vegas experience, Elvis ventured out on the road, the first venue being the Houston Astrodome. The concert was a massive sell-out, earning Elvis

The Comeback

$100,000. The Colonel was now convinced that touring could be as lucrative as the movies, with the added bonus of providing Elvis with a new high press profile and a boost in record sales. Elvis went back on the road almost permanently.

Over the next seven years, the singer was to visit 125 cities across North America and play over 1,000 concerts, every one of them a sell-out. That Elvis never toured Europe or Asia in these years was suspected to be due to the fact that the Colonel had anxieties regarding his legal status. The Colonel had entered the United States back in the 1920s and it was alleged that his entry had not been entirely above board. So long as he remained in the United States he was safe, but if he ever left the country immigration officers would examine his passport on re-entry, which might be a problem.

Nevertheless, the road tours were a phenomenal success made all the greater because no rock and roll star had ever made such a comeback before. A previous generation of singers, such as Sinatra, had always played to a wider audience than the teenagers of the 1950s who had idolized Elvis and nobody in the music business was entirely certain how a teen idol past the age of 30 should behave. However, it was Elvis who largely set the pattern that later rock stars would follow as they grew older. His outfits became increasingly bright and stereotyped but his movements on stage became more graceful and contained rather than implying raw aggression. Effectively he aged with his audience, while remaining young and dynamic enough in style to attract a new generation of fans. It was a masterful, and calculated performance.

Among the many venues played by Elvis during this period was the rather odd choice of the Houston Livestock Show and Rodeo in Texas. In his early days, Elvis had played country fairs and rodeos in plenty, but he had never been a star attraction. On more than one occasion he, Scotty Moore and Bill Black had simply played their instruments from the back of the pickup truck they had used to get them there. Now, however, Elvis was the star attraction and many of the onlookers had come to watch Elvis rather than the rodeo.

One of the viewers was rather disappointed by what followed. *'The back-up singers had been towed into place aboard a portable bandstand. They waited in place as the chuckwagon races were run around them. After a pause, during which policemen stood at parade rest around the perimeter of the area, Elvis appeared. Aboard a jeep, unimaginatively enough. While the bandstand slowly turned 180 degrees (the cheap seats never got more than a profile), Elvis worked his little heart out for about 30 minutes. The act was less than dynamite, although I can't truly think of an act in the business that could play that joint and expect to do more than survive. Presley does a Las Vegas headliner act. It's a good one, but heaven knows the rodeo is not the place to stage it. Less Presley's fault than the people who booked him there.*

'But you've seen lots of Las Vegas headliner sets just like it. It's odd to see an original making himself ordinary. The slicker Presley gets, the less interesting he is. If Presley could again sound as though he cuts records back in someone's garage, he could blow right out of the water any single act in the business. In his current incarnation, done up in sparkle-

OPPOSITE and BELOW
Elvis in his dragon jumpsuit. At one interview in the early 1970s he was asked if his large income and glamorous lifestyle constantly touring large cities, meant he was no longer the quiet, shy country boy he had always been. Elvis smiled and answered with another question, 'Shy country boy?', as he stood up to display himself in all his glory.

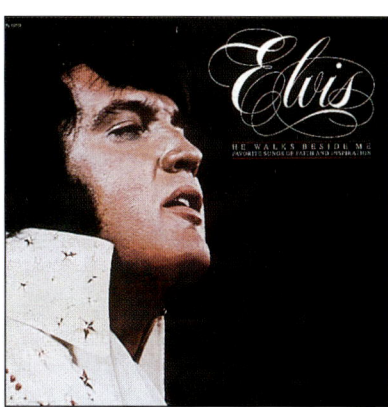

The Comeback

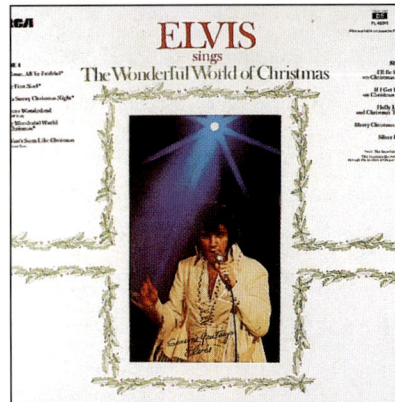

plenty jumpsuits, he looks and occasionally performs like the Oldest Osmond.' Although less than glowing in its comments, the review made no attempt to minimize the pure skill of Elvis as a stage performer and musician.

Although Elvis had abandoned the movies after *Change of Habit* and *Charro*, he could not help thinking that a feature film was still a major stage on which to display his skills to the fans. In December 1970, a new movie called *Elvis – That's the Way It Is* was released. The film was very different from his earlier efforts. Effectively, it was a documentary featuring Elvis on tour, largely in a format later known as 'fly-on-the-wall'. The movie was a huge success which, if anything, boosted demand for tickets for live shows.

Nor did Elvis neglect his recording career. The million-selling singles continued to appear with *In the Ghetto, Suspicious Minds* and *Don't Cry Daddy* in 1969, *The Wonder of You* in 1970 and *Kentucky Rain* in 1971. As well as live albums, Elvis spent a lot of time in the RCA Nashville studios and one of the most important of these sessions was the one which took place over a period of five days in June 1970. Elvis had obviously put a lot of pre-studio effort into the session with well rehearsed numbers and careful arrangements.

The songs ranged from country classics such as *Faded Love* and *There Goes My Everything,* to contemporary hits which included *Bridge Over Troubled Water* by Simon and Garfunkel, and took in the religious song *Only Believe* and the standard Elvis rock and roll *Got My Mojo Working*. The tracks were released as singles and on a number of albums over the following months. In another major session in May 1971, over 30 tracks were recorded over seven days. Again, there was a great range of styles and songs but with, this time, a distinctly more religious flavour. Indeed, two of the albums originating from this session were religious in content. The fall of 1971 saw *Elvis Sings the Wonderful World of Christmas* which had such great rock numbers as *Merry Christmas Baby* and *I'll Be Home on Christmas Day.* Later, in 1972, came *He Touched Me* which, in addition to the title track, featured *Amazing Grace, I've Got Confidence* and *Lead Me, Guide Me,* on which Elvis also played the piano backing.

In January 1972, the road outside Graceland was renamed Elvis Presley Boulevard. It was one of many honours to come Elvis's way as his career went from strength to strength. He was commended by successive presidents of the United States as a role model to the nation's youth, was honoured by law enforcement agencies across the nation and was given a high profile role in the fight against drugs by President Nixon.

With such a high media presence, Elvis had little hope of avoiding interviews entirely, though he never felt comfortable giving them. One of his stipulations was that he would talk about his music, his career and nothing else. Once when a reporter tried to get Elvis to express his opinions on a burning issue among liberal left-wingers, his response was both instructive and pure Elvis.

'What is your opinion of war protesters,' the reporter asked, 'and would you today refuse to be drafted?'

Elvis smiled and shook his head. 'I'd just sooner keep my personal views on that to myself. I'm just an entertainer. I'd rather not say.'

'But do you think other entertainers should also keep their views to themselves,' persisted the reporter, unwilling to let go without getting Elvis to say something controversial.

'Oh, no,' said Elvis moving, on to the next question.

Perhaps the greatest media success of these years was the great *Elvis: Aloha from Hawaii* television spectacular of January 1973. The journey from the mainland United States to the islands on 9 January, his arrival at the airport and journey to his hotel were all recorded on film and quickly edited together as a preview to the following television show. The show was intended to raise funds for a cancer research programme founded in honour of the Hawaiian musician Kuiokolani Lee, who had died of the disease. The show was beamed live from the islands on 14 January, after strenuous rehearsals and a warm-up concert two days earlier. Japan, South Korea, Australia, New Zealand, Vietnam, Thailand and the Philippines were able to see the show live, though time differences meant that Europe had to wait until the following day. NBC did not show the spectacular until three months later, by which time the concert had been heavily edited and songs from other shows inserted.

But while Elvis was enjoying massive public acclaim and learning to deal with the trappings of fame and fortune, his personal life was in trouble. Although he had bought a specially converted Greyhound bus, and a jet liner named *Lisa Marie* to carry his family and friends around with him, constant touring was beginning to put a strain on his relationships: Priscilla, in particular, was drifting away from him. In 1972, Priscilla met Elvis's karate instructor, Mike Stone. Before long it became clear that the two were growing close. Elvis, meanwhile, was spending time with the beauty queen Miss Tennessee, Linda Thompson. In October 1973 the marriage ended in divorce.

Elvis and Priscilla remained friends, however, and she remained a frequent visitor to Graceland or to wherever Elvis happened to be on tour.

By 1975 the concerts were still sell-outs, but RCA was not able to sell the live albums as profitably as before. As stage shows, the concerts inevitably contained large numbers of Presley classics and old songs which had appeared on albums before. RCA wanted Elvis to learn new songs and cut an entirely

BELOW
Elvis backstage before a concert. The concerts, tours and other public appearances began to take their full toll. The constant need to keep slim and trim, despite his eating habits, also caused problems, with a succession of crash diets beginning to sap his strength and damage his health.

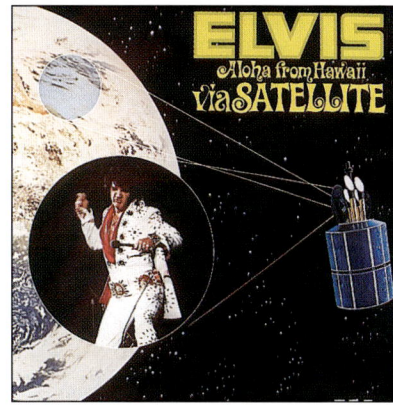

The Comeback

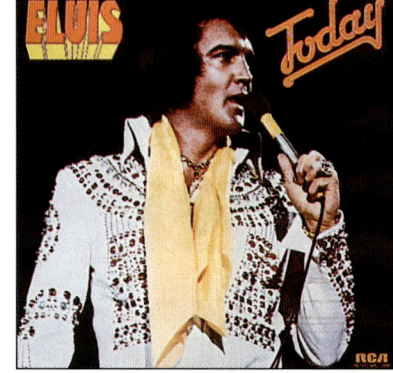

new album.

In March, Elvis attended the RCA studios in Hollywood for a three-day session, concentrating on producing Presley versions of songs which had already been hits for other artists. Among the titles recorded were *Susan When She Tried* (Statler Brothers), *Green, Green Grass of Home* (Tom Jones) and *I Can Help* (Billy Swan). The tracks were released as the album *Today TROUBLE* and sold moderately well.

But RCA was still not content and in February 1976 demanded yet more new material. Elvis was evasive and unwilling to work in RCA's studios, so the session was held in the studio at Graceland. RCA capitalized on the unusual setting by naming the album produced, *From Elvis Presley Boulevard, Memphis, Tennessee*. The session produced a group of songs which varied from outstanding to mediocre, some of the better songs being among the best Elvis achieved in the 1970s. A second session at Graceland in October 1976 was generally less successful. It did, however, produce *Way Down*, released as a single which did very well.

Part of the reason for Elvis's erratic recording output were his increasing health problems, being admitted to the Baptist Hospital in Memphis on several occasions for a variety of complaints. These included exhaustion, eye strain, pneumonia and a range of intestinal problems. Some of these ailments pointed to the underlying reasons for Elvis's physical deterioration during the 1970s: his diet and problems with his weight.

From childhood, Elvis had been devoted to the country cooking of the South, his favourite foods including hamburgers, grits, ham, corn pone, fried corn and okra and biscuits, as well as deep-fried sandwiches and other dishes originally produced by his mother. Coupled with a natural inclination to run to fat, this diet was proving disastrous. Elvis was gradually putting on weight, eventually reaching 224lb (102kg) when his normal weight should have been around 154lb. Rather than try to control his weight, Elvis binged on gigantic meals and frequent visits to favourite restaurants when not on tour. Then, just a few weeks before a tour was due to begin, Elvis would go on a crash diet which amounted to virtual starvation. Such a programme, repeated at regular intervals, could not be good for anyone's health, but Elvis compounded what was already a bad situation with prescription drugs.

For some time Elvis had been in the habit of taking stimulants to help him cope with disturbed sleep patterns developed as a result of being on the road. Now he added appetite suppressants, often accompanied by laxatives, to try to curb his famous appetite. This combination was most likely the cause of the intestinal problems which led to occasional hospitalization and which were also so painful (increasingly so as crash dieting became more frequent) that painkillers were added to the mix.

None of the drugs Elvis was taking was illegal, but their use in large quantities and in unconventional combinations was ruining his health. Elvis's doctor, George Nichopoulos, had been treating him since 1966 and had, in the early years, tried to encourage his patient to take up regular exercise, including racquetball, and to curb his craving for fatty foods. But his efforts proved fruitless. Dr. Nichopoulos began signing prescriptions for drugs and in one eight-month period prescribed over 5,000 doses of various medicines.

The fact that he was receiving from Elvis generous gifts, such as a Cadillac, as well as large payments, caused some of his fellow professionals to wonder if his judgement was being clouded. After Elvis's death, when the full story came out, Dr Nichopoulos was temporarily barred from practising medicine while an investigation was undertaken by the Tennessee Medical Board. Charges were brought, but the doctor was later cleared.

Although the public was largely ignorant of Elvis's health problems, and the reasons for them, his decline could not be concealed. In August 1976, a music critic attending a concert alongside 17,000 other fans wrote: *'Attending an Elvis Presley concert these days is like making a disappointing visit to a national shrine. Elvis strode on stage puffy faced and dressed in a gaudy costume with a six-inch belt, posed for thousands of instamatic flashcubes during a quick runthrough of CC Rider. He still*

ABOVE

Elvis attends a publicity drive to emphasize his global appeal. By the 1970s Elvis habitually wore dark glasses to protect his eyes from bright sunlight. His sleep pattern had settled to a routine of waking up in time for an evening concert, staying awake all night and sleeping during the day.

OPPOSITE

An exhausted Elvis showing the strains of touring and his growing problem with prescription drugs which was to darken his final months.

The Comeback

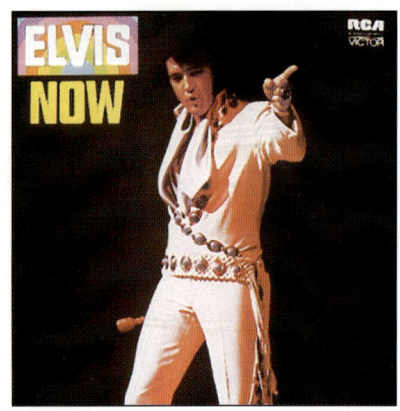

BELOW
A distracted Elvis after a show. The weight problems which plagued Elvis in his later life are clearly gaining the upper hand. His liking for down-home Southern cooking was legendary, as was his prodigious appetite.

has a remarkably strong, deeply resonant voice that, unfortunately, he displayed only rarely. He spent most of his time tossing scarves like Mardi Gras favors to the audience, shaking hands, receiving flowers and presents and kissing the women persistant enough to break through the throng to the stage and pull themselves up close enough to The King that he didn't have to lean over too far.

'Elvis pulled himself up momentarily when he launched into his current single Hurt, *singing with enough conviction to carry over into a pleasant but unchallenging version of* Ain't It Funny How Time Slips Away. *Then he had the house lights turned up to get a look at the "real show" – the undyingly loyal fans of every age screaming and scrambling in the hopes of possessing just one little piece of Elvis like a chip from a petrified forest. I wonder how many of those fans – who will surely claim that Saturday was one of the finest moments of their lives – noticed that after an hour-and-20-minutes show, there was no ovation for Elvis or the band. Just a crowded rush to the exits and the traffic jam waiting in the parking lots.'*

It was all a far cry from the dangerous teen star of earlier years. The comeback was at an end.

CHAPTER EIGHT
ELVIS LIVES

By 1977, Elvis was fast becoming a physical wreck. His concerts early that year were successful enough, and he performed competently, but no more than that. On 21 June he travelled to the Omaha Civic Auditorium to film a television concert for CBS.

The video shows Elvis clearly unwell. His face is puffy, his movements slow and at one point he has to be helped upright. During breaks in the music, when he speaks to the audience, he can barely mutter and mumble. But despite this, he manages to perform with power and authority. His voice was clearly undamaged by the failing state of his body and although the pictures are heart-rending, the integrity of the voice and his determination to go on are both testaments to Elvis and his courage.

After the show, Elvis returned to Graceland. He was due to go on tour that August, a prospect he did not relish; but there was some seriously bad news to be faced first. The previous year Elvis had fired Red and Sonny West after they had been a little too rough with fans on more than one occasion. In July 1977, a book written by the Wests appeared in print. It detailed the prescription drug-taking, the wild mood swings this created, and the declining physical state of the King.

The book *Elvis, What Happened?* was a great shock to Elvis. He had expected his old friends to maintain discretion in spite of losing their jobs – as Priscilla had done after the divorce. The reaction to the book was mixed. In some areas it was taken as proof that Elvis was finished, but in the Southern states, where Elvis had his roots and his most loyal following, there was a massive upswell of support. Bookshops refused to stock the book, and those who did found copies vandalized on their shelves. It was a hard time for Elvis: he knew he was in poor shape and was worried that his career might be at an end.

On the night of 15 August, Elvis could not sleep. He had played racquetball for some hours before sitting down at his piano to play some old favourites. Sometime after dawn he stopped playing and picked up a religious book. A few hours later, Ginger Alden – whom Elvis was planning to marry – found Elvis slumped on the bathroom floor. She called Joe Esposito, who had been Elvis's best man, but neither could

Elvis Lives

wake him. Dr Nichopoulos was called, and at once alerted local paramedics while he tried to revive his patient. The paramedics raced Elvis to the Baptist Hospital, but to no avail. At 3.30 p.m. he was pronounced dead, the immediate cause of death being heart failure. Exactly what underlying causes led to the death are not stated on the death certificate and have been the cause of conjecture ever since.

News of the death spread quickly: within an hour, a small crowd had gathered outside Graceland. By 6.30 p.m. the crowd had grown to over 20,000, standing in shocked silence at the news. One Elvis fan living in Memphis recalled the day. *'I used to hang out at a bar called the Poor and Hungry Café. The patrons were the young media, college kids, self-styled intelligentsia – you name it. On one wall hung the biggest black velvet painting of the King that I had ever seen. It was tacky and wonderful at the same time. I had a ticket to the concert Elvis was scheduled to give in Memphis that week. He had not performed in Memphis in a long time, so many of us were going together. Of course, it never happened. We just went to the P and H and drank ourselves silly and played* Heartbreak Hotel *over and over again on the juke box.'*

In Chicago, the news arrived as the newspapers were going to press. A reporter

recalled the scene: '*I was visiting the Chicago Sun Times where I was trying to sell some freelance articles. I was standing in the newsroom when a guy ran by yelling "Elvis is dead!". Seconds later a voice boomed across the newsroom "Stop the presses." It was a moment I'd only seen in the movies. To this day, I still get chills when I think of that editor ordering the* Sun Times*'s presses to stop.'*

The funeral was held a few days later at Forest Hills Cemetery, Memphis, where Gladys Presley had also been buried. The two bodies were later transferred to a private garden of meditation at Graceland because it was thought that visitors to the grave might disturb the cemetery. By the time the cortège pulled out of Graceland, Memphis was swollen by 200,000 visitors who had come to pay their last respects. President Jimmy Carter paid an official tribute when he remarked, '*Elvis Presley's death deprives our country of a part of itself. He was a symbol to the people of the world of the vitality, rebelliousness and good humour of this country.*'

But although Elvis was dead, his adoring fans refused to relinquish him. In a phenomenon quite unlike anything that had gone before, the Elvis Presley legend and the business associated with it has continued to thrive, even to grow, since his death. No other entertainer has been afforded such a mass of posthumous fame and fans who continue to adore him. The ultimate credit must go to Elvis himself, for without his talent, good humour and sheer skill, his music would have been lost to the world. Since his death it has been Priscilla Presley who has controlled official Elvis memorials and who has been as jealous as Colonel Parker in preserving Elvis's memory from malicious gossip or unworthy criticism.

The centre of the Elvis phenomenon is, of course, Graceland. Under the terms of Elvis's will, the majority of his possessions were left to his daughter, Lisa Marie, with Priscilla as trustee until she reached 25 years of age. After Elvis's death there was great pressure on Priscilla to sell up, to capitalize on the outpouring of grief by selling Elvis's personal effects and to invest as much money as possible for her family's well-being. But Priscilla refused to do this. She gives her reason, in her own words: 'No, I don't want Lisa, when she's

Elvis disembarks from his private jet liner, *Lisa Marie*, while on tour. Leading the way is Ginger Alden with whom Elvis had an affair after his marriage to Priscilla failed.

25, to say "Where's my Dad's stuff".'

Instead, Priscilla created Elvis Presley Enterprises and invested the $500,000 left by Elvis in opening Graceland to the public. The house and grounds were altered and converted to contain the expected flow of visitors in safety and comfort. Numbers exceeded anyone's expectations: in just 38 days Priscilla had recouped the entire investment. It would be difficult to think of any other business which could say as much. The business was intended to take care of Elvis's relatives as well as being a memorial to him; any of his many cousins who wanted a job were given one, and many still work on the estate in various capacities.

Twenty years after Elvis's death, Graceland attracts over 700,000 visitors every year. The estate has moved on apace since the first visitor paid to walk through its doors. Instead of merely being able to take a look at the King's home, visitors are treated to an entire 'entertainment experience'. Guests are given headsets which play recordings of Elvis, as well as personal recollections of Priscilla and an informative commentary is provided as a bus takes visitors from the main gates to the mansion.

Outside the mansion itself are other attractions. The automobile collection features the original 1955 pink Cadillac Elvis bought his mother with his first big earnings, together with other Cadillacs and a selection of Harley-Davidsons and three-wheeled superbikes. There is also the Cadillac with customized gold-plated dashboard that Elvis drove the day before he died. The aircraft on view includes the *Lisa Marie* jet liner on which Elvis toured, as well as

the much smaller *Hound Dog*, a private executive jet for more informal travel.

As far back as 1955, Colonel Parker was licensing the Elvis image to sell a range of trivia from badges to posters. In 1956, there were 70 such items, including glow-in-the-dark photos and bermuda shorts. This lucrative sideline eventually boomed to include official and pirated goods such as fake Elvis hair, pen-knives, watches, mugs, key-rings, plaster busts, thimbles, and even table-lamps, and continued throughout Elvis's life and beyond. In recent years, Elvis Presley Enterprises has made determined efforts to stamp out the tackier souvenirs by enforcing legislation, copyrighting

Flanked by members of the 'Memphis Mafia', Elvis arrives at another city during his strength-sapping tours of the mid-1970s. His battle with his weight caused many problems, not the least of which were the crash diets, followed by bingeing which put a terrific strain on his liver and kidneys.

Elvis's image, as in the case of the late Princess of Wales.

There has been little attempt, however, at cracking down on the more genuine and sincere testimonies to the memory of the King. In fact, this would not only be counter-productive to the memory of Elvis, but also virtually impossible. There remains so much genuine devotion to him that thousands pay tribute in their own way. When Elvis died there were an estimated 38 Elvis impersonators earning a living from singing his songs at private parties or appearing at charity events. Today there are an estimated 11,000.

Perhaps the most bizarre, and most impressive are the famous Flying Elvii, based in Las Vegas. The ten-man team travel to fairgrounds, parties and other events throughout the United States to perform their act, jumping from heights of up to 15,000 feet (4,572metres). Depending on the weather, the Elvii skydive down to 2,000 feet, forming and reforming into various patterns as they fall. When they open their parachutes and set off the smoke trails, the Flying Elvii steer their chutes to weave in and out of one another, leaving intricate smoke trails in their wake before landing on a marked target. At night, the Flying Elvii wear specially adapted jumpsuits with dozens of lights attached. Once on the ground, the men shed

Elvis Lives

Elvis, followed by Ginger Alden, meets some of his fans on his way to a show. The trademark sun glasses and stand-up collars were by 1974 very much in evidence whenever Elvis appeared in public.

their parachutes to sign autographs, partake in photocalls and generally mingle with the crowd.

Among the more popular attractions of the Flying Elvii is the all-included Elvis Wedding in Vegas package in which a happy couple, intent on getting married in Las Vegas get everything laid on by the group, including an 'Elvis' as best man, while others serve as witnesses and the whole team fronts up at the ceremony before performing their stunning act.

To cater for this demand there are numerous shops selling Elvis-style sunglasses, jumpsuits and black wigs. Ties emblazoned with pictures of Elvis are another popular item, alongside T-shirts and even replica jumpsuits. Companies producing products unlicensed by Elvis Presley Enterprises are usually careful to say so: 'Elvis Presley is a trademark of Elvis Presley Enterprises and is in no way associated with these products', runs a typical disclaimer.

Other companies do not need to be so careful: Paramount, after all, owns the copyright on the movies that Elvis made for them, subject to royalty payments to his estate. In 1997, Paramount decided to re-release several of his movies onto the home video market. Sales boomed and the release proved to be every bit as successful as when the films first appeared in the cinemas.

In 1997, Mattel Incorporated teamed up with Elvis Presley Enterprises to launch a double act on the market, linking two of the United States' most powerful icons. The two-doll set, *Barbie Loves Elvis,* was launched at

Graceland in August by a Barbie look-alike. The Elvis doll wears a regal gold lamé jacket with black crêpe collar and cuffs and a guitar in imitation of his classic 1957 Elvis Homecoming concert in Tupelo. Barbie, meanwhile is dressed in what is basically 1950s style with a pink angora sweater and scarf and black flannel skirt.

As with all these items, it is the Elvis fans who provide the market for them and keep the interest going. In 1996 a campaign was launched over the internet to have 8 January declared a national holiday in the United States. To back up their bid, the fan clubs stated that 'Elvis Presley personifies the American Dream'. They emphasized that he was a poor boy, born in obscurity, who became the King of Rock and Roll, amassing a great fortune and never saving a penny. Elvis had it all and died from a surfeit of cholesterol, drugs and rock and roll. Elvis was no draft-dodger: when his country called, he gladly served in the army though it meant temporarily forsaking a successful career. Perhaps it is just as well that the suggestion from fan clubs that every school should offer its pupils an Elvis lunch of deep-fried peanut butter and banana sandwiches has not been implemented.

Those same fans continue to buy Elvis records in huge numbers: by 1998, more than one billion had been sold worldwide. In 1992 RCA and Elvis Presley Enterprises decided to work out exactly how many discs had been sold and to ascertain which should be awarded gold, platinum and multi-platinum awards. After months of work, the U.S. sales figures were finally calculated, and in 1995 Elvis was posthumously awarded no less than 110 such awards. The figures for overseas sales are still incomplete, especially those for the early years when detailed sales records were not always maintained. Even so, the list puts Elvis at the top of the all-time record sales list. The winning margin is truly breathtaking. In 1995, when the Elvis list was completed, the Beatles stood in the number 2 slot with just 45 gold or platinum discs.

But perhaps the most amazing aspect of the posthumous Elvis phenomenon are the recurring rumours that he did not in fact die in 1977. Within a few months of his death, sightings of Elvis began to be reported all over the United States, and later worldwide. The sightings were simply of a man who resembled Elvis – other witnesses reported that the man behaved like Elvis as well.

One witness reported, *'I saw Elvis at the local diner down here in Overbrook. He was drinking a diet coke and eating some fried chicken. When he left he thanked the cook for a mighty good meal and said he sure was thankful. He paid with a hundred-dollar bill and told her to keep the change. He then got in a 1953 Chevy Bel-Air custom turquoise and white auto. It had tinted windows and he said to the driver "Let's go Bubba", and he was gone.'*

A more recent sighting from 1994 also reported Elvis behaving in typical fashion. *'I was driving just outside Durham, NC, when my car started bucking. I pulled off the road in a rather remote area. I was working under the hood looking for the trouble when a 1959 Cadillac Sedan with tinted windows pulled alongside me. The driver asked if he could be of any assistance. I informed him I believed I had the situation under control. As the Cadillac pulled away, I noticed through the back window that was down three of four inches, seated in the back seat of the car was Elvis Presley. He was wearing sunglasses and had a slight grin on his face as the Caddy pulled away.'*

As early as 1981 Kirsty McColl was able to have a hit with the single *There's a Fella Down the Chip Shop Swears He's Elvis...*, and everyone knew what she was singing about. It was not long before conspiracy theories to account for Elvis's survival began to circulate. These have ranged from the relatively simple idea that Elvis was fed up with his lifestyle, with the book by the Wests and the continual pressures of life on the road. He therefore faked his death, either using a waxwork dummy or substituting the body of another man who died at the time, and took off with his money. According to this theory he is now living quietly in some remote area, but he cannot hide his true character and sometimes gives himself away by ordering home-style Southern cooking or bursting into song.

The more elaborate conspiracy theories tend to centre around Elvis's army career and his role in anti-drugs campaigns. According to this, Elvis was involved in a major drugs bust, either through the FBI or army intelligence. Because of the highly secretive nature of the business, Elvis had to be spirited away under the Witness Protection Scheme to live a new life under an assumed name.

Although the evidence produced to back up these various theories (and there are many more) is largely fictional, obscure or unverifiable, there is one piece of evidence that most quote which is very true. On Elvis's tombstone and death certificate, his middle name is given as 'Aaron', but throughout his entire life he used the spelling 'Aron'. It is claimed that the reason for the change of spelling was so that nobody could be accused of the federal crime of falsifying a death. If Elvis Aaron Presley never existed, nobody could fake his death.

So persistent did these rumours become, that Graceland was forced to issue an official explanation. Elvis was named after a friend of his father's, Aaron Kennedy. However, Vernon chose to spell the name Aron to match the name of Elvis's stillborn brother Garon. For this reason Elvis used the Aron spelling throughout his life. The doctor who registered the birth, however, did not know this and used the Biblical, and more usual, spelling of the name on the birth certificate. A few months before his death, Elvis decided to revert to the Biblical spelling and began to inquire how he could change his name under Mississippi state law. When he learned he was already registered as Aaron, he gave up the quest and began using the new spelling.

That these theories and sightings continue to proliferate more than 20 years after Elvis's death indicates that his appeal is as great and enduring as ever. Before Elvis, there was no rock and roll and it would seem that there will never be another like him. For Elvis is still with us in spirit, on film and, most importantly, in his music.

Elvis the man may have died, but Elvis the legend lives on.

INDEX

Alden, Ginger 101, 103, 106
Allen, Steve 42
All Shook Up 52
Arnold, Eddy 34, 36, 43
Atkins, Chet 37, 40

Baby I Don't Care 51
Baby Let's Play House 30, 31
Beaulieu, Priscilla 58, 60, 61, 62, 78, 81, 82, 84, 91, 97, 101, 103, 104
Berle, Milton 16, 40, 41, 42
Black, Bill 20, 26, 29, 30, 36, 37, 95
Blue Hawaii 76, 77
Blue Moon of Kentucky 21, 24, 25
Blue Suede Shoes 40, 41, 44

Cash, Johnny 46
Change of Habit 71, 92, 96
Charro 7, 65, 91, 96
Cramer, Floyd 37, 86
Curtiz, Michael 52, 53

Don't Be Cruel 42, 46

Egan, Richard 45, 69
Elvis: Aloha from Hawaii 97
Elvis Christmas Album 23, 52
Elvis – That's the Way It Is 96

Flaming Star 75, 78
Flying Elvii 105, 106
Fontana, D.J. 30, 37

G.I Blues 35, 66, 67, 68, 74
Girls, Girls, Girls 71, 78
Gleason, Jackie 38
Good Rockin' Tonight 23
Got a Lot of Livin' to Do 52
Graceland 32, 47, 50, 51, 57, 62, 65, 67, 78, 81, 82, 98, 101–104, 107
Grand Ole Opry 23, 24

Harbor Lights 20
Heartbreak Hotel 10, 37, 38, 40, 41
He Touched Me 96
Hillbilly Cat and the Blue Moon Boys 22, 25, 30
His Hand in Mine 76
Hound Dog 40, 41, 42

I Apologise 20
I Don't Care if the Sun Don't Shine 23
I Don't Hurt Anymore 20
I Forgot to Remember to Forget Her 31
I Got a Woman 37
I Love You Because 20
I'm Counting on you 37
It's Now or Never. 67, 68
I Want You, I Need You, I Love You 42
I Was the One 37, 38

Jailhouse Rock 51, 52, 61, 78, 79, 81, 82
Just a Little Talk with Jesus 46

Keisker, Marion 8, 9, 10, 19, 58
King Creole 52, 53, 54, 58, 74, 78, 82

Lacker, Marty 18, 48
L. C. Humes High School 10, 17, 19, 48
Lewis, Jerry Lee 36, 46, 62
Louisiana Hayride 24, 25, 27, 29
Love Me Tender 18, 41, 42, 45, 68, 69
Loving You 41, 47, 51, 52, 60

McColl, Kirsty 108
Matthau, Walter 53, 82
'Memphis Mafia' 50, 58, 60, 105
Memphis Recording Service 8, 9, 19
Milkcow Boogie 29, 31
'Million Dollar Quartet' 46
Moore, Scotty 20, 21, 22, 23, 24, 26, 29, 30, 36, 37, 95
Mystery Train 30, 31, 58

Neal, Bob 25, 30, 31, 34, 35, 36, 48
Nichopoulos, George 99, 102

Old Shep 14, 19, 23, 52
Orbison, Roy 36

Paradise – Hawaiian Style 71, 77, 83
Paralysed 47
Paramount Pictures 44, 52, 68, 75, 106
Parker, Colonel Tom 31, 32, 34–36, 38, 40–44, 51, 54–58, 60–62, 67, 73, 75, 77, 78, 81, 83, 86, 87, 91, 92, 94, 103, 104
Peace in the Valley 52, 53
Peer Music 9, 10
Perkins, Carl 36, 46
Phillips, Sam 8, 9, 10, 19, 20, 21, 22, 23, 30, 35, 36, 46, 48, 50
Presley, Gladys 8, 9, 11, 12, 13, 14, 17, 22, 35, 42, 47, 50, 56, 57, 103
Presley, Jesse Garon 11, 108
Presley, Lisa Marie 86, 103
Presley, Vernon 9, 11, 12, 13, 14, 35, 47, 50, 58, 60, 68, 73, 108

RCA Victor 10, 21, 36, 37, 38, 40, 50, 55, 57, 58, 67, 96, 97, 98, 107
Reno Brothers, The 45, 69
Return to Sender 57, 78
Rock-a-Hula Baby 77
Rodgers, Jimmie 14

Shake, Rattle and Roll 38, 40
Sinatra, Frank 68, 94
Snow, Hank 31, 34, 36
Sullivan, Ed 42, 43, 47
Sun Records 9, 21, 22, 29, 31, 35, 36, 37, 46, 48, 55
Suspicious Minds 91, 96

Teddy Bear 41, 47
That's All Right 20, 21, 22, 23, 24, 25, 58
That's When the Heartaches Begin 8, 23

Tommy and Jimmy Dorsey Show 38, 40
Tomorrow Night 31
Tonight is So Right for Love 67
Treat Me Nice 51
Trying to Get to You 31
20th Century Fox 45, 75

Wallis, Hal 44, 45, 61, 66, 68, 74, 76
Welcome Home Elvis 68
West, Red 17, 18, 19, 48, 50, 101, 108
WHBQ 22, 34
Whitman, Slim 22, 23, 31
Wild in the Country 75, 76
Without You 9, 10
Wooden Heart 67

You're a Heartbreaker 30
You're Right, I'm Left, She's Gone 30, 31, 58